"Dr. Reay answers the question that many parents in the throws of high conflict divorce ask, 'Am I being the victim of parental alienation?' She will effectively answer the question in a succinct manner with real life examples that allow the reader to empathize with other victims of alienation. Secondly she answers the question, 'What do I do about the alienation?' with exercises that provide the reader with added insight and direction to help prevent being further victimized. Her book is comprehensive and easy to read and understand."

Douglas Darnall, Ph.D.,
Author, *Beyond Divorce Casualties: Reunifying the Alienated Family*

*"In **Toxic Divorce: A Workbook for Alienated Parents** Dr. Kathleen Reay has created an easy to read interactive workbook for parents and a primer for both mental health and legal professionals as they all seek to understand the complexity of the continuum of alienation. Reay highlights the differences between the normal preferences created in everyday family life, the dynamics that lead to justifiable estrangement, and the insidious impact of the unjustifiable processes that provoke the pathology that is Parental Alienation Syndrome. But more! This text offers hope to both child and parent victims of these processes as well as perspective to professionals by introducing all concerned to strategies aimed at an ultimate resolution of the heartache created by the processes of alienation."*

Glenn Ross Caddy Ph.D., A.B.P.P., F.A.P.A.,
Clinical and Forensic Psychologist, Fort Lauderdale, Florida,
Director, The International Institute of Psychology and Behavioral Science

"Parental alienation is a particularly pernicious outcome of dysfunctional family relationships. Almost every extended family member is involved and affected in one way or another—both the preferred parent and the alienated parent; the maternal and paternal grandparents and other relatives; and all the children. In this book, Dr. Kathleen Reay has focused on the alienated parent. Although these situations are complex and there are no easy answers, Dr. Reay provides empathic support for the alienated parent and much advice that is practical, doable, and realistic. The format of **Toxic Divorce** *as a workbook prompts the reader to think through the author's suggestions and develop his or her own plan of action. While alienated parents will benefit most from this book,* **Toxic Divorce** *will also be useful for other family members, friends, adult children of parental alienation, mental health professionals, and legal professionals."*

William Bernet, M.D., Professor, Department of Psychiatry,
Vanderbilt University School of Medicine,
Nashville, TN and author of *Parental Alienation, DSM-5, and ICD-11*

"A seminal book that advances our understanding of parental alienation. Parents, clinicians, legal professionals, and collaborative professionals alike will be thankful for Dr. Reay's guidance and expertise in resolving a highly complex family dynamic that's been tearing families apart for generations and leaving children with scars of emotional abuse. This book will also launch Reay into a modern day pied piper because of its counseling value to mental health professionals around the world."

Joseph Goldberg, Parental Alienation Consultant & Founder, Canadian Symposium
For Parental Alienation Syndrome, www.CSPAS.ca

*"***Toxic Divorce** *is a clear and insightful view into the potential dangers and pitfalls of divorce at its worst. This book will help the reader not only identify what is happening to them but help them heal from the devastating effects of a toxic divorce and parental alienation. This is a must read for anyone overwhelmed by their divorce and feeling caught off guard by what is happening to them."*

Barb & Rick Nischalke, Co-Founders, Keeping Families Connected
www.keepingfamiliesconnected.org

TOXIC DIVORCE

A Workbook for Alienated Parents

Kathleen M. Reay, Ph.D., D.A.A.E.T.S.,
Diplomate, American Academy of Experts in Traumatic Stress

Library and Archives Canada Cataloguing in Publication

Reay, Kathleen, 1960-
      Toxic Divorce: A Workbook for Alienated Parents/ Kathleen Reay.

Includes bibliographical references.
ISBN 978-0-9869178-0-6

1. Parental alienation syndrome--Handbooks, manuals, etc.
2. Children of divorced parents--Psychology--Handbooks, manuals, etc. I. Title.

RJ506.P27R43 2011   618.92'89   C2011-904713-6

If you would like to publish sections of this book, please contact
the publisher for permission.

Published by:

Kathleen M. Reay, Ph.D.

250-276-9467

Email: drkathleenreay@gmail.com

www.parentalalienationhelp.org

Editing by Carole Audet

Cover and content design by Ingrid Koivukangas

Photographs: Morguefiles.com - Photographers:
   • Scott Liddel • Mary R. Vogt • Kenn W. Kiser • Ariadna • Anita Patterson • Nestor Romero
   • Mary K. Baird • Phaedra Wilkinson • Michael Connors • Dee Golden • Jade Krafsig
   • Ali Lhoshjam • PuraVida • grietgriet@live.be • dzz@mail.ru • kamuelaboy@gmail.com

Love's Chain

Can we not hear our children crying
as our relationships are left dying?

The harms we choose, the words we say
later in life come into play.

Things we've said add to that they know,
And in future relationships this may show.

What we say children take as truth,
So please be honest and not steal their youth.

Tell truths of love always from your heart.
This allows for healing to start.

Listen up and hear your children's voices.
They deserve their freedom of choices.

Don't let your thoughts cause children pain

instead keep adding links to your love's chain.

~ Ronald G. Boroski

Table of Contents

Forewords by Jayne A. Major, Ph.D. and Carol Maker, LCSW

Dedication

I dedicate this book to all the wonderful children and youth that I have had the pleasure of working with throughout my clinical career. Each and every one of them has been so tragically affected and caught in the middle of unnecessary family alienation. I also dedicate this book to all the wonderful alienated parents, both men and women whom I have also had the pleasure of working with. Thank you so ever much for trusting me and working with me to help make positive changes in your lives. I will forever be indebted for all the lessons that you taught me about this type of family abuse. Your stories will never be forgotten in both my memory and my heart.

Foreword

Foreword by Jayne A. Major, Ph.D.

Toxic Divorce is a powerful contribution to the literature related to the serious problem of parental alienation or parental alienation syndrome. Targeted parents experience the worst torture imaginable. They helplessly watch their beloved sweet children turn into monsters that spit at them, curse and are so contrary that the simplest chore like setting the table or getting ready for bed is a hateful experience. How can this happen? How do you explain that in a short period of time a child can lose his or her critical thinking abilities regarding their once nurturing parent and cross over to be on the side of the meanest, cruelest and most unhealthy parent? They protect the cruel parent and discard the healthy parent. *Toxic Divorce* helps us understand this phenomenon and points the reader in a positive direction to show what can be done about it.

Helpless parents wonder and ask, "What am I supposed to do?" Few people understand why their children are acting with such rebellion when there doesn't seem to be a cause for it. Parental alienation has always existed in divorcing families, but it first began to become a more widespread problem in divorces in 1980. Kathleen Reay, Ph.D.

has done a masterful job in explaining the phenomenon, the history and controversies around parental alienation and parental alienation syndrome.

Toxic Divorce has enormous value as a workbook. Dr. Reay points parents in the right direction regarding handling the distressing emotions of a targeted parent. Parents who are facing the awfulness of parental alienation are encouraged to process their fears, anger and confusing thoughts in constructive ways. Parents are coached to understand counterproductive thinking and how to get rid of it. All targeted parents are overwhelmed with powerlessness, grief and loss, often having no idea where to turn. One of the most valuable parts of *Toxic Divorce* is how to cope with the grief and loss and the myriad insults to their sensibilities in what is right and what is wrong.

Toxic Divorce is a must read for mental health professionals. Families where parental alienation and parental alienation syndrome exist are not a matter of business as usual; entirely different therapeutic skills are needed. For example, the heads of these toxic families have been described as cult leaders. The children and other family members who refuse to be followers of the cult leader are treated with cruelty. Children literally have their critical thinking taken away and are forced to align with the cult leader. This becomes a desperate survival issue for them. They no longer understand that the targeted parent and relatives that represent one half of their heritage still love them. They are helpless in that they are unable to help the child to maintain anything close to an objective reality about their family. Without exposure to healthy people, brainwashed children become increasingly bizarre, accusing the target parent of a host of terrible behavior that they have never done. Therapists who are not trained in the special techniques that these families require often fall into the trap of believing the alienating parent and the brainwashed child and make the egregious mistake of contributing to the problem. There are few therapists that have had advanced training in how to handle these cases and the need is great.

If this is a specialty that interests you, you could make a powerful contribution to the distressed families that are affected by a serious dysfunction that far too many divorcing parents experience.

Another word about parental alienation, for a long time now there are many who have taken upon themselves to demonize Dr. Richard Gardner and distort facts about parental alienation to a ridiculous degree. While they think that they are helping, they are instead greatly contributing to the problem.

Jayne A. Major, Ph.D.

Major Family Services, Inc.

Los Angeles, California

www.stopparentalalienation.org

Foreword by Carol Maker, LCSW

This workbook provides up-to-date scientific knowledge, understanding and a tremendous amount of direction and tools to help parents and professionals deal with the burgeoning phenomenon of Parental Alienation (PA) or Parental Alienation Syndrome (PAS). As an alienated child, an alienated parent, and a therapist specializing in trauma, I can attest to the suffering involved in any kind of alienation, be it triangulating, scapegoating, bullying or shunning. Identifying parental alienation after a divorce can be helpful in treating family members and decoding the source of their suffering. However, sometimes it's hard to distinguish between PA and the more severe PAS.

Since PAS is a combination of the brainwashing and the child's contribution to the alienation of the parent (a position seemingly fraught with unidentified guilt) traditional forms of psychotherapy will likely not be effective. Without accountability for their contribution to the injustice, or awareness of the guilt they may be suppressing, justification for the alienation resists any type of logic, accountability, or healing. A therapist unfamiliar with the land-mines in understanding this dynamic may innocently, and unintentionally, aggravate the situation by supporting the alienation.

An alienated parent will feel many emotions that range from rage to despair, and underneath it all runs a river of shame and horror. When the alienation is not corrected, the alienated parent, like the child, can become lost in a vast array of emotions. The challenge is to move out of the matrix of insanity, but how can the parent make the choice to escape knowing that the child is left behind, still lost in that matrix?

Underneath all the crazy making, both the alienated child and the alienated parent have a deep and desperate desire for someone to protect them, to help them find a way out of the nightmare. To increase the possibility of change, the common practice of "taking sides" or "remaining neutral" must be replaced by understanding the dynamics of triangulation, scapegoating, bullying, shunning, all forms of passive aggression, *along with a keen awareness of the power differentials inherent in all these dynamics.* Only then can there be transparency, honesty, accountability and true healing. For the alienated parent, the journey out of the erroneous belief that they alone can heal the relationship is a spiritual one. This is a painful grieving and "letting go" of the dream they once held for their life while, somehow, staying open to a miracle. The exercises in *Toxic Divorce* are a beginning to this painful and difficult process.

Dr. Reay's research, demonstrating the correlation between levels of PAS and psychological distress of the adult children of divorce, speaks to the tragic price that is paid when effective interventions are not available to these families. It is time for "outsiders"—whether it be friends, family, the legal system or therapists—to intervene to stop the effects of this multi-generational tragedy.

Carol Maker, LCSW
Inner Courage LLC, Portland, Oregon
www.innercourage.com

Acknowledgements

From its conception, writing this workbook took many grueling hours to complete. I wish to thank the many individuals who have contributed in so many different ways to help make it a final product and success.

To start with I wish to thank my wonderful husband, Murray who has been so very supportive and caring throughout my educational and career journeys. Without you, it's likely that I would not have reached the many goals and aspirations that I've sought and accomplished to date. Thanks to my two wonderful daughters, Tara and Kristy, who have taught me so much about life and especially about the importance and value of family. Although it's an illusion to believe that there is such a thing as a "functional" family, it's my honest opinion that the four of us closely meet a dictionary's definition. I also feel very blessed that none of us have personally experienced the anguish associated with the topic of this book.

I am honored to receive an endorsement from Jayne A. Major, Ph.D., a highly respected authority on divorce, child custody, parental alienation, and parental alienation syndrome. She consults with attorneys, judges, mental health professionals, and parents in the United States and abroad.

Dr. Major is the author of numerous books and has written many academic articles. She is also the founder of Breakthrough Parenting Services, Inc., a non-profit organization providing outstanding parent education classes for those impacted by divorce and child custody issues for over twenty-five years. Thank you Dr. Major for taking the time from your very busy schedule to read the entire manuscript and write the Foreword. I have learned much from you, have been enriched from our discussions and look forward to experiencing a life-long professional relationship with you.

I express gratitude to Ronald G. Boroski, a good friend who has undergone significant challenges and obstacles in his life. He is an amazing poet, and I'm very proud to include a poem that he wrote relating to Parental Alienation Syndrome.

Recently, I had the opportunity to meet Carol Maker online, a psychotherapist in private practice in Portland, Oregon. She described some of her tragic life history of being an alienated child and an alienated parent. She had only learned there were labels for parental alienation and parental alienation syndrome not long before we initially connected. After conversing with each other via email several times and providing her a copy of my manuscript, Carol very graciously offered to write a second Foreword for my book. Carol, thank you for taking the time to write your thought-provoking testimonial and for sharing some of your personal life with those who read this book. I'm so glad we met and am looking forward to more engaging conversations on this very serious topic.

Special thanks go to William Bernet, M.D., Douglas Darnall, Ph.D., and Glenn Ross Caddy, Ph.D. for taking the time to review my manuscript and for offering positive feedback and support. The cumulative contributions that each of these esteemed experts on high-conflict divorce and parental alienation have made to the research community with peer-reviewed scientific articles, chapters, and books are outstanding. Words cannot express how appreciative I am to receive your support and encouragement.

Special thanks is also extended to Joseph Goldberg, the Founder of the Canadian Symposium for Parental Alienation Syndrome and a parental alienation consultant who also took time out of his very busy schedule to read my manuscript and offer positive feedback and support.

Enormous gratitude is extended to Carole Audet, my professional author's assistant who has been instrumental throughout the manuscript preparation, editing, publishing and marketing process. Carole, I am so blessed to have had this incredible opportunity to work with you. Your expertise, professionalism, energy, creativity, conceptual thinking, dependability, conscientiousness, and outstanding organizational and time-management skills have not gone unnoticed. I look forward to working together on another book on this subject matter in the future.

I am also greatly indebted to Ingrid Koivukangas who did a phenomenal job designing the cover and interior pages of this book. Ingrid, you did an amazing job choosing all the images for the book's cover and interior pages. Thanks for the great formatting work you did, too. Your passion, inspiration, creativity, enthusiasm, professionalism, reliability, efficiency, and organizational skills are greatly cherished. I look forward to working with you on another project in the future, too.

Much of what I have learned about the personal side of parental alienation has been from the many children and families that I have had the pleasure and opportunity to work with in my private counseling practice. Their stories have been an inspiration to me and I am deeply grateful. I am also deeply grateful to the many families who took part in my research study conducted on the long-term effects of parental alienation syndrome. At that time, numerous individuals traveled long distances within the region to participate. Additionally, many participants reportedly chose to be a part of my research study for a significant reason: they wanted to make a special contribution to the field of research because their lives have been so deeply affected in varying ways by their parents' divorce. Each and every participant in my research study as well as the hundreds of clients seen in private practice have helped me gain tremendous knowledge and understanding of complex family dynamics, in particular parental alienation and its associated effects, during the divorce process and long afterward.

Writing this book has turned out to be a catharsis for me. In trying to understand the various aspects of parental alienation I have reconciled myself to the fact that although so many children suffer there's much we can do in society to stop it. This process has only reinforced what I know already: family means everything.

D. K. R.

Introduction

In the 1980s, Dr. Richard A. Gardner, a child and forensic psychiatrist, championed a child custody litigation phenomenon called Parental Alienation Syndrome (PAS). Since that time, the PAS phenomenon has gained increased recognition in both the mental health and legal fields. For well over four decades, parental divorce has been determined as the cause of a variety of significant physical, emotional, academic, and social difficulties in children and adolescents. Moreover, high-conflict between divorcing or divorced parents, including the PAS phenomenon, is a noteworthy risk factor for children and adolescents.

This workbook is the first of its kind for alienated parents and is divided into three parts. Part One will provide the knowledge and understanding you need to personally deal with the ramifications of PAS or to help those who do. Thus, from a broad perspective this book is written for a wide array of readers including those directly affected by PAS as well as for extended family members, significant others, counselors, social workers, psychologists, psychiatrists, child custody evaluators, family mediators, general practitioners, pediatricians, family law lawyers, judiciary, police officers, school administrators, school teachers, and policy makers.

After reading Part One from a personal perspective, you will have a clear understanding of the differences between parental alienation and parental alienation syndrome. You will also be able to distinguish the varying degrees of alienation and its long-term effects. Psychological characteristics of alienated children including some developmental issues and the psychological characteristics of alienating parents will also be covered. From a mental health perspective, Part One will offer more tangible and scientifically valid data to lend support to the potential inclusion of PAS in the upcoming edition of the Diagnostic and Statistical Manual of Mental Disorders (5th ed.) (DSM-V). It will facilitate the recognition of treatment modalities for parents who have experienced the effects of PAS. From a legal perspective, it will offer more tangible and scientifically valid data to lend support to judicial decisions in child custody litigation matters. These chapters include the most up-to-date findings from the scientific community.

Part Two of this book will provide step-by-step directions and strategies for alienated parents to help battle PAS. This workbook teaches methods that have been shown to be very beneficial for individuals suffering from various forms of anxiety, panic, depression, jealousy, stress, anger, abandonment, trust, shame, and guilt issues. Given that alienated parents tend to experience one or more of the above-noted difficulties, the strategies provided in this book can be a great source of help. Moreover, this book can also help alienated parents improve their self-esteem, handle stress better, become less anxious and fearful, while increasing their confidence in dealing with PAS. The strategies offered in this book come from cognitive-behavior therapy (CBT), which has been proven in numerous studies to be the treatment of choice for these types of difficulties.

CBT has two components: identifying and changing the distorted thinking patterns that maintain anxiety, depression, stress, anger, etc. (cognitive therapy), and desensitizing anxiety through exposure to feared situations (behavior therapy). The relative emphasis put on each of these depends on the nature of the alienated parent's difficulties. In some instances, an alienated parent may need to work both on changing his/her thinking patterns and exposing him/herself to the situations that are feared. The most powerful tools to help deal with the effects of PAS are education, acknowledgement, kindness, caring, compassion, as well as the will and commitment to help stop it from destroying the lives of so many children and families.

Part Three of this book will offer additional important information for mental health professionals, alienated parents, and interested others. Clinicians will have a greater understanding and appreciation for the need to get specialized training in this type of work. You will learn about some controversial issues about parental alienation that have greatly contributed to the problem of it not being fully recognized to date. Historical developments relating to divorce and custody that led to the formation of PAS will also be provided. You will also learn the most up-to-date findings on the proposed diagnostic criteria for parental alienation that have been submitted to the DSM-V Task Force of the American Psychiatric Association.

All in all, this workbook can serve one or more beneficial purposes. Please keep in mind that this book is not intended to act as a substitute for psychiatric or psychological treatment services provided by a qualified mental health professional. If you believe you and your child are being alienated, I encourage you to seek support from a trained and experienced mental health professional in this field. A highly trained mental health professional will have the ability to confirm whether PAS is truly occurring in your situation. Moreover, an experienced clinician can help you decide whether self-directed cognitive-behavior therapy is appropriate for you at this time or whether it would be beneficial to seek some other form of professional help instead. The workbook is intended to help you in the following ways:

In the event you are feeling a little uneasy about seeking professional help from a qualified mental health therapist, this workbook will help you learn as much as possible about PAS and help validate the struggles you may be experiencing. Individuals are invited to use this workbook in conjunction with ongoing psychological or psychiatric treatment by a qualified mental health professional. Your therapist may also want to read this workbook to assist in the role of advocate, coach, guide, or advisor.

Additionally, your written responses in this workbook can be used to help you and your attorney in an attempt to argue your case for PAS. In working with the legal community, I have found that attorneys are very appreciative when their clients write notes or journal their experiences with PAS. It makes the attorneys' jobs a little easier! Therefore, I encourage you to share this book with your attorney and feel free to photocopy your written responses for legal purposes.

Lastly, you may be reading this book because you have a family member or friend who has undergone a toxic divorce and/or may be undergoing family alienation. This workbook can help you seek a greater understanding of PAS in order to provide valuable support. Targeted parents need trusted family members and friends to support them during this very difficult time.

PART ONE

"What's done to children, they will do to society."

~Karl A. Menninger, MD

(1893-1991)

Chapter One
Why Should I Learn about PAS?

Contrary to popular media portrayals of divorce, the majority of divorces in the United States and Canada do not implicate acrimonious and long-drawn-out disputes over child custody and access ... Unfortunately, high-conflict divorces, or what I like to refer to as "toxic divorces", encompass roughly 10 percent of all divorcing families in the United States and Canada and are considered extremely harmful to the children and the adults concerned...

... high-conflict divorces, or what I like to refer to as "toxic divorces", encompass roughly 10 percent of all divorcing families in the United States and Canada and are considered extremely harmful to the children and the adults concerned ...

Contrary to popular media portrayals of divorce, the majority of divorces in the United States and Canada do not implicate acrimonious and long-drawn-out disputes over child custody and access. As a matter of fact, approximately 90 percent of divorces are non-contested and never require formal court interventions (Maccoby & Mnookin, 1992; Richardson, 1996). In contested cases, child custody and access issues are less likely to be addressed compared to division of property, and spousal and child support (Richardson, 1996). Consequently, parents who mutually choose to engage in low-conflict divorces are believed to cause minimal harm on their children's physical and psychological well-being (Pearson & Gallaway, 1998). Unfortunately, high-conflict divorces, or what I like to refer to as "toxic divorces", encompass roughly 10 percent of all divorcing families in the United States and Canada and are considered extremely harmful to the children and the adults concerned (Maccoby & Mnookin, 1992; Richardson, 1996). This means that in the United States alone, the courts see protracted and repeated toxic divorce litigation cases that involve the lives and well-being of at least two million children (Duryee, 1992; Johnston & Roseby, 1997).

In the 1980s, Dr. Richard A. Gardner, a child and forensic psychiatrist, championed a child custody litigation phenomenon called Parental Alienation Syndrome (PAS). Since that time, the

PAS phenomenon has gained increased recognition in both the mental health and legal fields. By 2002, there had been no less than seventy-two rulings that cited PAS in law courts in countries throughout the world including the United States, Canada, Israel, Australia, Germany, Great Britain, and Switzerland (Berns, 2006; Gardner, 2002a, 2002b, 2002c, 2003, 2006; Gottlieb, 2006; Leitner & Kunneth, 2006). Beginning in early 2000, the PAS satisfied the necessary criteria for admissibility in certain courts of law in the United States and all of Canada.

The type of alienation described in this workbook is not normal in intact families. Yet, PAS is not listed in the DSM-IV (American Psychiatric Association, 1994) or what is commonly referred to as the Bible of Psychiatry and Psychology in my field. Prior to his death in May 2003, Dr. Richard Gardner strongly petitioned the American Psychiatric Association to list it in the upcoming 5th edition of the Diagnostic and Statistical Manual. Gardner's followers—primarily consisting of researchers, mental health professionals, legal professionals, politicians, and parenting organizations—continue to support the inclusion of PAS in the DSM-V. PAS is a burgeoning phenomenon. Whether this is the first time you've heard the term PAS or not, there's plenty of information following that will increase your knowledge and understanding of it.

Important Note:

It is ultimately up to you to decide when you feel ready to complete the self-directed worksheets. No one can make this decision for you including a mental health therapist, physician, family member, attorney, or friend. No one can change your situation for you and you are truly the only person you can change. You cannot change the alienating parent's thoughts, feelings, or actions nor can you change those of your alienated child. As the saying goes, "You can lead a horse to water but you cannot make it drink." This expression

... No one can change your situation for you and you are truly the only person you can change. You cannot change the alienating parent's thoughts, feelings, or actions nor can you change those of your alienated child. ...

holds a lot of truth about your alienating ex and your alienated child. One of the purposes of this workbook is to help validate the realities and effects of parental alienation. You will have the opportunity to evaluate your own unique personal reality as well as learn various types of counterproductive thinking patterns that can affect your overall functioning. Therefore, this workbook can help you become skilled at seeing some differences between the reality of being an alienated parent and various types of counterproductive thinking that can get in the way. By choosing to alter some of your own counterproductive thoughts, negative feelings, and behaviors while receiving support from professionals, friends, extended family, and the judicial system, there is reason for hope and optimism that this work will help influence change and help you and your child break free from PAS.

... this workbook can help you become skilled ... and help you and your child break free from PAS ...

When you're ready to use this workbook, please respond to the following questions for your own clarification:

Time for Self-Reflection

List some reasons why you think it is important to learn about PAS:

_____

_____

_____

_____

_____

_____

_____

How do you plan to use this workbook?

_____

_____

_____

_____

_____

_____

If a mental health therapist or other professional recommended this workbook for you to use in conjunction with your therapy sessions, how do the two of you plan to get the most out of using this book? What have you both mutually agreed to do?

_____

_____

_____

_____

_____

_____

Why do you think it is important to complete the exercises in each chapter?

_____

_____

_____

_____

_____

_____

_____

What might happen if you choose to move too quickly through the workbook without giving yourself generous time to practice the skills taught?

_____

_____

_____

_____

_____

_____

_____

What are your goals for doing this work?

_____

_____

_____

_____

_____

_____

_____

_____

_____

_____

_____

_____

Additional notes:

_____

_____

_____

_____

_____

_____

_____

_____

_____

_____

_____

_____

_____

_____

_____

_____

Chapter Two
What is PAS?

*Some of you may have heard the term
parental alienation (PA) used.
If so, you may have wondered,
"What on earth is the difference
between PA and PAS, if anything?"
Well, there are distinct differences
between the two terms.*

D r. Richard A. Gardner introduced the PAS phenomenon in a 1985 published article called *Recent Trends in Divorce and Custody Litigation.* Here's his definition for it:

> The parental alienation syndrome (PAS) is a disorder that arises primarily in the context of child-custody disputes. Its manifestation is the child's campaign of denigration against a parent, a campaign that has no justification. It results from the combination of a programming (brainwashing) parent's indoctrinations and the child's own contributions to the vilification of the target parent.

... you may have wondered, "What on earth is the difference between PA and PAS, if anything?"

Some of you may have heard the term parental alienation (PA) used. If so, you may have wondered, "What on earth is the difference between PA and PAS, if anything?" Well, there are distinct differences between the two terms. The general term parental alienation entails any situation or event in which a child or youth can be alienated from a parent. A number of contributing factors can encompass the definition for PA such as the following:

- Parental verbal abuse
- Parental mental abuse
- Parental emotional abuse
- Parental physical abuse
- Parental sexual abuse
- Parental rejection & abandonment

- Parental neglect
- Parental mental illness (for example, major depression, bipolar disorder, anxiety, a personality disorder, etc.)
- Parental chronic illness or chronic medical disability such as a traumatic brain injury
- Parental criminality
- Inadequate parenting skills such as being overly punitive, intimidating, chronically angry and having unrealistically high expectations of children
- Children or adolescents who are hooked into cults and brainwashed to become alienated from a parent
- Children who are abducted by a parent
- Children who witness domestic violence
- Parental alcohol abuse/dependence, which can be combined with any of the above contributing factors
- Parental substance abuse/dependence, which can be combined with any of the above contributing factors
- Both parents may engage in alienation tactics
- Can occur in intact families and in toxic divorce cases

... True PAS necessitates that there is an identifiable parent who is programming the child against the other parent...

Here's the confusing part: PAS is one subtype of PA in which an identifiable parent systematically programs one or more children or youths in the same family against the other parent who has been a good, loving parent prior to the alienation occurring. True PAS necessitates that there is an identifiable parent who is programming the child against the other parent and the alienated child or youth manifests some or all of the eight manifestations discussed later in this chapter, whereas PA does not necessitate the identification of a specific programmer. In PA cases, both parents can be responsible for creating the alienation. In PAS cases, the alienating parent is generally the custodial parent who holds the most power and control over the child or youth. PA is legitimate justifiable alienation because some form of abuse, neglect, partial or total absence of parenting occurred to bring about alienation in the child. Estrangement tends to occur in the latter situations. PAS is legitimate unjustifiable alienation because there is no reason for it and the child and target parent had a good, loving relationship prior to its start.

> Parental Alienation is legitimate Justifiable Alienation
> Parental Alienation Syndrome is legitimate Unjustifiable Alienation

With respect to PAS, Dr. Gardner formulated eight primary manifestations of symptoms, which may or may not be present in every situation. They are:

1. The child aligns with the alienating parent in a campaign of denigration and hatred against the alienated (also referred to as the target) parent, with the child making active contributions.

... With respect to PAS, Dr. Gardner formulated eight primary manifestations of symptoms, which may or may not be present in every situation ...

2. Rationalizations for denigrating the alienated parent are often weak, frivolous, or absurd.

3. There seems to be no ambivalence in the child's feelings toward the target parent; thus, animosity toward the alienated parent is demonstrably severe.

4. The child states that the decisions to reject the alienated parent are the child's own (referred to as the Independent Thinker phenomenon).

5. There is an automatic, reflexive support by the child for the alienating parent.

6. The child expresses a guiltless disregard for the feelings of the alienated parent.

7. The child borrows from various subject matter and jargon of the alienating parent. Thus, the child's denigration of the target parent has a distinct rehearsed quality.

8. The child's animosity extends to the alienated parent's extended family and friends.

Although the eight manifestations of PAS are typically triggered during high-conflict child custody battles, PAS can also be precipitated during other divorce disputes including, but not limited to, child support issues, property division issues, remarriage, and financial arrangement issues.

It is not uncommon to hear about child abuse and neglect reports in PA and PAS cases. Protecting children from abuse and neglect is a societal responsibility. Each and every one of us has a responsibility and duty to report any incidence of suspected or disclosed child abuse at any time. You do not need to have evidence or actual knowledge of abuse when you make a report; all you need is reasonable cause, suspicion, or belief based on your observations. To get assistance or report abuse in the U.S. or Canada, call the Childhelp National Child Abuse Hotline at 1-800-4-A-CHILD (1-800-422-4453). You can also call your local child welfare agency directly. Depending on where you live, this agency may be called Child Protection Services, Children and Family Services, Child Welfare Services, Human Welfare, or the Department of Social Services. The contact number for your local child welfare agency in the U.S. can be found online at http://www.childwelfare.gov and in Canada at http://www.protectchildren.ca. Call 911 or your local law enforcement agency if you believe it is an emergency situation. If the allegation of child abuse cannot be proven, you will not get into trouble for making the report. Anyone reporting in good faith (with a reasonable belief) may not be criminally prosecuted or sued in civil court for libel, slander, defamation, invasion of privacy, or breach of confidentiality.

...Protecting children from abuse and neglect is a societal responsibility. Each and every one of us has a responsibility and duty to report any incidence of suspected or disclosed child abuse at any time...

Unfortunately, but true, both false allegations of abuse and virtual allegations of abuse are also generally seen in PAS (Cartwright, 1993; Gardner, 1987, 1992b, 1994; Rand, 1997a). It's not uncommon to see false sexual abuse allegations made by an alienating parent and an aligned child against a target parent in PAS cases (Gardner, 1987, 1992b, 1994). Rand (1997a) found that many alienating parents suspect that their children have been physically and/or sexually abused by their ex-partners, yet the ex-partners vehemently deny their suspicions and no objective evidence supports it. Alienating parents may also project blame onto their ex-partners for other actions that they perceive as neglectful or abusive. It's important to note that anyone who knowingly or recklessly makes a false report of child abuse or neglect is not protected from prosecution or civil suit.

Virtual allegations of abuse are also commonly seen in toxic divorce cases whereby the alienator may insinuate, imply, suggest, hint, intimate, or indicate that the other parent has abused their child but it's not true (Cartright, 1993). Here are a couple of examples: A mother who insinuates sexual abuse by the father by alleging that he had shown the child a pornographic movie which in fact was just a child's cartoon rented from a local video store. An alienating father falsely hints that his ex-wife physically abused their daughter on a weekend visit when in fact the child was accidentally hit and bruised on the arm from another child throwing a tennis ball at school.

... "When true parental abuse and/or neglect are present, the child's animosity may be justified, and so the parental alienation syndrome explanation for the child's hostility is not applicable." Gardner (2006, p. 5) ...

It's important to note that in instances where true parental abuse and/or neglect are found, the PAS label must not be employed. Gardner (2006, p. 5) stated the following: "When true parental abuse and/or neglect are present, the child's animosity may be justified, and so the parental alienation syndrome explanation for the child's hostility is not applicable."

As you can see PA and PAS are very complex topics. Both PA and PAS have been used interchangeably throughout the years. Hopefully, this chapter has helped clarify that both terms have distinct meanings. It's important to keep in mind that alienation not only can occur by parents, but mental health experts, physicians, attorneys, teachers, grandparents, stepparents, and others can easily alienate. Further, PA is not officially recognized as a syndrome by the American Psychological Association or the Canadian Psychological Association. Nonetheless, both bodies do recognize PA as a behavior that generally occurs during the separation and divorce process. An experienced, well-qualified mental health professional will offer specific treatment for the various subtypes of PA including PAS.

Kim's Experience of PA

Kim was ten years old when her mother, Alice, left their family and moved into an apartment with a new boyfriend. Kim's father, Dan, initiated the divorce process right away because he felt fed up. Kim refused to spend any time with her mother. Alice believed Dan had put Kim up to not wanting to see her. Alice and her boyfriend hired an attorney who in turn referred her to see me. I also met with Kim and Dan alone on a few occasions. It was both Alice and her attorney's hope that I would be able to help convince the judge that Kim should be court-ordered to see her mother. After conducting a comprehensive assessment of the situation, it became very clear that my written report to the attorney and possible testimony in court would not favor Alice. It became evident that Alice was suffering from a combination of alcohol dependence and a severe chronic psychiatric disorder. Kim described her mom as very cold, distant, and unloving throughout her childhood. She also described experiencing significant shame, rejection, humiliation, threats, and spankings by Alice. Dan described feeling bullied and intimidated by his wife for years. Similar to other abusive parents, Alice was not willing to acknowledge her responsibility for the serious difficulties in her relationship with Kim or Dan. Alice had no problem accusing Dan of damaging her relationship with Kim. There was no evidence that Dan was denigrating Alice or engaging in any other characteristics

> *... It became evident that Alice was suffering from a combination of alcohol dependence and a severe chronic psychiatric disorder. Kim described her mom as very cold, distant, and unloving throughout her childhood....*

commonly seen in true PAS cases. Kim's alienation did not meet the criteria for PAS but certainly did meet the criteria for PA. Her alienation was significantly warranted by her mother's behaviors. It was only natural for Kim to feel reluctant, scared, and unwilling to have a relationship with her mother. Further, Kim did not demonstrate any other characteristics related to PAS. Kim's personal choice to suddenly avoid her mother after she left the family home is the type of parent-child scenario that tends to become alienated even in the absence of separation and divorce.

Lydia's Experience of PAS

"I have not seen my two daughters, ages six and nine, for almost three years. My girls may hardly know me now. Yet we had incredible mother-daughter relationships prior to this nightmare. My husband and I divorced because we didn't communicate well. It ended up that we didn't sleep together for the last year of our marriage. My husband left us for another woman. That relationship didn't last long though.

... Upon separation, it was my hope that he and I would be able to sit down together with the kids and explain to them in little people's language that daddy and I were no longer able to live in the same house together. ...My husband refused to do that. ...

Upon separation, it was my hope that he and I would be able to sit down together with the kids and explain to them in little people's language that daddy and I were no longer able to live in the same house together. I also wanted to emphasize that it wasn't their fault and weren't to blame. My husband refused to do that. Instead I overheard him tell the girls while I was in the kitchen that the separation was happening because I was a bad mommy and none of them deserved to be around someone like me. They were all too good for me.

One day while I was at work, my husband purposefully packed the kids' belongings at our house, picked them up from the babysitter's and moved them into his new house on the other side of town. He used every possible measure to prevent me from seeing them.

The last time I was able to speak to my six-year-old was over the phone approximately three months after the separation. Our then three-year-old said she never wanted to see me again because they were all too good for me. Several times, she told me I was a bad mommy and my ex was a nice daddy. It ripped me apart.

I haven't been able to see my nine-year-old since that time either. Over the phone, she was very argumentative and rude. I couldn't believe it was the same child. She also described never wanting to see me. She even told me I should move out of town—there was no use me staying here. She suggested I move to Cambodia. Do many six-year-olds even know where Cambodia is?

Our then six-year-old mentioned that she remembered me spanking her hard on her bottom when she was one. She said she had bruises on her bum and it hurt for two days. She also said I used to freak out a lot. I attempted to tell her those accusations were not true. I told her how much I love her and said I've never freaked out nor spanked her. Instead, I have always done my best to talk gently and calmly. I also said she was given time-outs, when necessary. Her response was, "liar, liar pants on fire". She also said that she knows I make $35,000 a year and should be paying daddy some child support. Just before the end of our phone call, our then six-year-old told me that another reason that I'm a bad mommy is because I bought her an ice-cream cone right after the last ballet lesson I took her to. She said I shouldn't have done that because it was too close to dinner-time.

Two days after my last phone call with both children, I received an unexpected visit from a social worker from a local child welfare agency because my ex reported that I had gone 'out of my mind with erratic and outlandish behavior' and had threatened him with physical violence. He told them that he was in great fear of our daughters' safety if they were in my care. He also filed legal papers and got a temporary restraining order for three weeks while child

... I haven't been able to see my nine-year-old since that time either. Over the phone, she was very argumentative and rude. I couldn't believe it was the same child. She also described never wanting to see me. She even told me I should move out of town—there was no use me staying here. ...

welfare did an assessment. His allegations were proven false but he still tells people in our community that I'm a threat to our children and wants permanent sole custody. Even though there's no longer a restraining order, he's done everything possible to keep me away from the children. Our oldest daughter's school won't even let me be involved in her education or events.

I've attempted to get counseling for our children but my husband won't let me. He's fired five lawyers to date and our child custody battle worsens each time. We can't get anywhere because of his lies, manipulation and so many court adjournments. My lawyer hasn't been very helpful and I can't afford to pay any more legal bills. I may have to represent myself from now on. My husband will have a great laugh when he sees that. I'm completely at my wit's end and see no end to this mess. I feel like I may have lost my girls forever. It's horrible."

Lydia's story is a very sad case of PAS. She had a loving relationship with both children prior to the separation. Her ex's behaviors demonstrate that he systematically programmed the children. Both young daughters quickly aligned with him in a campaign of denigration and hatred toward her. The children have also demonstrated many active contributions in denigrating her. The children's animosity toward their mother is very severe. Lydia's daughters have given trivial and absurd explanations for why they no longer want to have a relationship with her. From a developmental perspective, some of the things Lydia's daughters have said to her are not possible for young children to be aware of. Even Lydia's three-year-old child at the time was engaging in the "nice daddy" versus "bad mommy" dichotomy. Clearly, both girls have mimicked things they've heard from their father, including subject matter that children should have no business knowing. Unfortunately, Lydia also experienced false allegations of threatening physical violence toward her husband and possibly harming her children. Like many

... I've attempted to get counseling for our children but my husband won't let me. He's fired five lawyers to date and our child custody battle worsens each time. We can't get anywhere because of his lies, manipulation and so many court adjournments. ...

alienated parents and children, a despicable cycle of abuse of power has taken place not only by her ex, but by various societal structures including the legal system.

Dale's Experience of PAS

"For nearly ten years, my father forced me to stop loving my mother. I was twelve years old when my parents separated and the alienation began. At first I knew it was wrong but I felt I had no choice but to become swept up by my father's backbiting remarks about mother. I now recognize after undergoing therapy in adulthood that he filled my head with hateful ideas about her. My father would say she was stupid, ignorant, a bad mother, and didn't love any of us. I finally felt so convinced by his denigrating remarks about her that I talked the same way to others about her. I didn't want to ever see her again. I also stopped having contact with my maternal grandparents, aunts, uncles, and cousins. I hated her so much. I hated them all except for my father. He was perfect. I never felt guilty about my own thoughts and feelings about each parent.

... For nearly ten years, my father forced me to stop loving my mother. I was twelve years old when my parents separated and the alienation began. ...

My father passed away two years ago from cancer. It was extremely difficult because I loved him so much. My mother and I had the opportunity to reconcile a couple of years after my father's death. She found me on Facebook and slowly we began to rebuild our relationship. During therapy sessions with my mother recently, I learned that she constantly tried to maintain contact with me through phone calls and letters. She also mailed gifts for my birthdays, Christmas, and Easter. My father obviously did a pretty good job not letting me know that any of this had occurred. Instead, he'd remind me on birthdays, Christmas, and Easter what a horrible parent my mother was for forgetting me and not sending gifts.

My therapist also helped me see that my mother has always been a caring, considerate, thoughtful, and loving parent. Family has always meant everything to her. Prior to the separation, she juggled many roles including being a full-time mother, a part-time nurse, a great cook, and she attended all my sporting events. Although my mother and I will never truly be able to make up for all those lost years, I am grateful that we have reconnected."

In Dale's case, true PAS occurred because he aligned with his father in a campaign of denigration and hatred against his mother. Dale made active contributions in denigrating his mother. There was no ambivalence in his feelings toward his mother. Dale demonstrated an automatic, reflexive support for his father whom he thought was perfect. And, Dale's animosity extended to his mother's extended family. ❧

... Dale demonstrated an automatic, reflexive support for his father whom he thought was perfect. And, Dale's animosity extended to his mother's extended family ...

Time for Self-Reflection

List some reasons why you believe that Parental Alienation or Parental Alienation Syndrome is occurring in your own family or a family you care about:

_____

_____

_____

_____

_____

_____

_____

_____

_____

_____

_____

_____

_____

_____

_____

_____

_____

_____

_____

_____

_____

_____

_____

_____

_____

_____

Struggling with PA or PAS

In the event that you perceive experiencing PA or PAS, please take the time to fill out this exercise below:

Briefly describe the story of your own struggle of being an alienated parent:

_____

_____

_____

_____

_____

_____

_____

_____

_____

_____

_____

_____

_____

_____

_____

_____

_____

_____

_____

_____

_____

_____

_____

_____

_____

_____

Briefly describe what you perceive your alienated child or children are struggling with:

_____

_____

_____

_____

_____

_____

_____

_____

_____

_____

_____

_____

Describe some of your worst experiences with PA or PAS:

_____

_____

_____

_____

_____

_____

_____

_____

_____

_____

_____

_____

_____

_____

_____

_____

_____

Describe the progression of PA or PAS from the beginning until now. In what ways have your circumstances changed during the weeks, months, or years?

_____
_____
_____
_____
_____
_____
_____
_____
_____
_____
_____
_____
_____
_____

How has the alienation impacted you physically? (For example: I experience sleep difficulties, low energy, fatigue, eating difficulties, muscle tension, abdominal distress, nausea, agitation, etc.)

_____
_____
_____
_____
_____
_____
_____
_____
_____
_____

How has the alienation impacted you mentally and emotionally? (For example: I am grieving multiple losses; experiencing anxiety, depression, anger; difficulties coping with the stress; difficulty communicating with others; feeling numb, isolated, rejected, betrayed, etc.)

_____

_____

_____

_____

_____

_____

_____

_____

_____

_____

_____

_____

How has the alienation impacted you socially? (For example: I do not feel like doing things that I used to do prior to the beginning of PA or PAS; I am experiencing a lot of isolation and am spending little or no time with friends and family members; I have little patience with annoying situations at work, etc.)

_____

_____

_____

_____

_____

_____

_____

_____

_____

_____

How has the alienation impacted you economically? (For example: I am working fewer hours; My doctor put me on a medical leave from work due to my difficulties; I had to quit going to school part-time; I had no choice but to sell the house and other major assets to pay legal bills; I am in a lot of debt from this high-conflict court battle and legal bills, etc.)

_____

_____

_____

_____

_____

_____

_____

_____

How has the alienation impacted you spiritually? Your responses can be positive and/or negative. (For example: I no longer go hiking outdoors like I used to do; I couldn't care less about staring at the evening stars anymore; I no longer believe in God or some other Higher Power; I have a stronger belief in God or some other Higher Power now; I haven't the energy to practice meditation; I stopped praying because there's no use; My situation is hopeless; I pray much less now; I have been praying more since the alienation began; I do not attend church; I attend church regularly now; I do not read any inspirational books; Inspirational books have been very helpful recently; I have shared my PA or PAS story with my Rabbi; I have not shared my story of alienation with a member of the clergy, etc.)

_____

_____

_____

_____

_____

_____

_____

How might your life be different if you were to overcome some or all of the above listed effects of PA or PAS?

_____

_____

_____

_____

_____

_____

_____

_____

_____

_____

Additional notes:

_____

_____

_____

_____

_____

_____

_____

_____

_____

_____

_____

_____

_____

_____

Chapter Three
Don't Jump to Conclusions

Before moving further into the topics of PA and PAS, there's an important point to be made. Please don't jump to conclusions that PA or PAS will always be present. There may be one or more reasons why a child refuses to have contact with a parent that doesn't involve PA or PAS....

... It's normal for a child or youth to prefer one parent over the other in intact, blended, separating, divorcing, and divorced families. ...

Before moving further into the topics of PA and PAS, there's an important point to be made. Please don't jump to conclusions that PA or PAS will always be present. There may be one or more reasons why a child refuses to have contact with a parent that doesn't involve PA or PAS. The general term contact refusal is defined as "behavior of a child or adolescent who adamantly avoids spending time with one of the parents during or after the divorce process that cannot be considered a mental condition, a syndrome or a disorder" (W. Bernet, public presentation, May 28, 2011). There are at least seven different reasons why contact refusal may occur that aren't necessarily related to PA or PAS. The following are brief descriptions of each.

Normal Preferences

It's normal for a child or youth to prefer one parent over the other in intact, blended, separating, divorcing, and divorced families. It's also normal for an older child or teenager to prefer to hang out with friends and/or to prefer to attend school or recreational activities rather than spend time with one or both parents in intact, blended, separating, divorcing, and divorced families. Beyond separation, it's normal for a child or youth to prefer to spend more time at one parent's home than the other parent's. This is especially the case when the child remains in the family home.

For example, within two weeks of his parents' separation, fifteen-year-old John preferred to stay at home with his father for the weekend rather than visit his mother at her new home. John's preference is a normal response when the parental separation process begins. This cannot be described as PA or PAS. However, if John's refusal to visit his mother becomes unremitting and he begins to express a hatred toward his mother, then a thorough evaluation needs to be made to consider whether his behaviors have become pathological.

What can parents do when a child refuses to visit the other parent in the early stages of parental separation? There is no one specific intervention. Bernet (public presentation, May 28, 2011) suggests that in some instances it's advantageous to offer the youth a flexible schedule and in other instances it's advantageous to offer a set schedule. Warshak (2010c) advises that it's advantageous for both parents to recognize that it's okay for their son or daughter to act this way in the beginning of the separation process but if it persists after two consecutive occasions, then it's necessary for both parents to determine why the child is refusing contact with the one parent and for both parents to communicate to the child that contact with both parents is necessary and healthy for all parties involved.

... What can parents do when a child refuses to visit the other parent in the early stages of parental separation? There is no one specific intervention. ...

Loyalty Disputes

It's normal for a child or youth to experience feelings of guilt regarding parental divorce and wish for parents to reunite. It's also normal for a child or youth to feel bad about neglecting a parent, feel concerned and worry about the absent parent, as well as grieve for the absent parent. In these kinds of situations, it's important for both parents to tell the child or youth that there's no need to worry about either parent, encourage the child or youth to have fun when in the company of either parent, and insist that the child never blames him/herself for the divorce (W. Bernet, public presentation, May 28, 2011).

Anxious and Stressed Child

It's normal for toddlers to feel anxious and stressed when a primary caregiver says goodbye even when separation or divorce hasn't occurred. In these instances, a child who has a loving attachment will naturally cry, perhaps have a temper-tantrum, and not want to physically let go of the parent who leaves. Even though it's difficult, separation anxiety is a normal stage of development and usually diminishes as the child grows older. When parents separate and divorce, it's only natural that their toddler will continue to experience separation anxiety if it began prior to the separation, or it may resurface or begin at this time.

Some children experience persistent and excessive anxiety, fears, and uncertainties about separation as they grow older and have difficulties leaving one or both parents to go to school or take part in other activities. In these cases, it's possible that the child is experiencing separation anxiety disorder or panic disorder and may require help from a mental health therapist. For these same children, when parents separate or divorce their symptoms and complaints will likely increase. Additionally, children who have witnessed a lot of parental fighting in toxic divorce cases are at an increased risk of developing separation anxiety disorder. As Dr. Bernet (public presentation, May 28, 2011) points out, "When a child loses a relationship with Parent A, fears losing Parent B, then the child clings to Parent B and develops separation anxiety. When this occurs the child resists leaving home to visit Parent A."

The best intervention is for both parents to have a lot of patience, understanding, compassion, and use effective coping strategies to help relieve their child's anxiety and worry. It's helpful for both parents to develop a special goodbye ritual such as a goodbye kiss, a unique wave, or a high-five symbol, to help reassure the child that leaving is only temporary. For an anxious child, it's advantageous to keep surroundings familiar when possible and to help the child get

... When parents separate and divorce, it's only natural that their toddler will continue to experience separation anxiety if it began prior to the separation, or it may resurface or begin at this time. ...

accustomed to new surroundings by involving him/her in the process of setting up this new space. The goal is to help the child become less anxious in both households. Cognitive-behavioral therapy involving the child and both parents is beneficial and in extreme but rare cases, the short-term use of anti-anxiety medications may help the child (W. Bernet, public presentation, May 28, 2011).

Reversal of Parenting Role

During the separation and/or divorce process, some parents feel extremely debilitated and experience a particular form of regression in which they become too dependent on one or more of their children. These parents tend to feel very depressed, troubled, anxious, lonely, and experience difficulties taking responsibility for themselves or their children.

On occasion, a role reversal occurs in which the child becomes the parent's caregiver, confidant, and perhaps even therapist. The child begins to experience faulty logic and takes on an excessive amount of responsibility. The child loves both parents but tends to not want to leave the debilitated parent alone for fear of what may happen in his/her absence. As such, the child may not want to visit the other parent even though that parent hasn't done anything to warrant the exclusion. In these rare cases, parental alienation is not occurring. Nonetheless, if proper interventions are not put in place quickly, two likely outcomes can occur. One, it's possible that the child will end up resenting the debilitated parent and possibly feeling used, abused, and/or neglected. In this case, parental alienation will likely develop. The child could potentially end up refusing to have any contact with the debilitated parent. Or, two, if the debilitated parent continues to communicate to the child his/her excessive neediness and inability to be left alone, then the child may ultimately feel discouraged from seeing the other parent. A seven-year-old girl I once worked with ended up telling her father that

> *... On occasion, a role reversal occurs in which the child becomes the parent's caregiver, confidant, and perhaps even therapist. The child begins to experience faulty logic and takes on an excessive amount of responsibility. ...*

she hated him and refused any further contact with him because her mother desperately depended on her for so much. In these rare cases, the seeds of parental alienation can quickly sprout.

Effective interventions are necessary otherwise the child is at an increased risk for PA or PAS to develop. It's important for the debilitated parent to seek help from an experienced mental health professional as soon as possible. It's not healthy for any child or youth to become robbed of his/her childhood or adolescence and have to play a parenting role. Under these circumstances, the child or youth will likely need some assistance from a therapist, as well.

Tenacious Child

Some children are strong-willed, tenacious, determined, inflexible, oppositional, and stubborn. I recall one parent describing her six-year-old daughter as a force to be reckoned with since infancy. According to this mother, her daughter baulked at being fed with spoons, bottles, changing clothes, and numerous other activities that other children at the same age just naturally engaged in without any screaming matches.

When parents separate or divorce, the above-noted types of personality characteristics tend to intensify in these children (W. Bernet, public presentation, May 28, 2011). These children usually become more oppositional, angry, resentful, inflexible, and stubborn and may prefer to spend more time with one parent over another or spend more time in the original family home than at a parent's new home. When these types of behaviors occur, the child's parents tend to become even more frustrated, which aggravates the problem. The opposition is generally seen in both households (W. Bernet, public presentation, May 28, 2011).

In some circumstances, depending on whether the child fits the diagnostic criteria, he or she may be diagnosed with oppositional

... It's important for the debilitated parent to seek help from an experienced mental health professional as soon as possible. It's not healthy for any child or youth to become robbed of his/her childhood or adolescence and have to play a parenting role. ...

defiant disorder and the parents and child benefit from the help of an effective mental health provider. In these instances, parental alienation is not present as long as the preferred parent does not reward the child's avoidance of the other parent (W. Bernet, public presentation, May 28, 2011).

Conflict Dodging

Unfortunately, but true, some divorcing or divorced parents choose to continue to act like foes and engage in ongoing, unremitting hostility in front of their children. Typically, these parents fight over financial issues, property issues, parenting issues, unresolved feelings, a need to be right, and other types of power and control issues, among other things. In the vast majority of cases, the children love both parents yet feel so caught in the battle (Warshak, 2010c). These children tend to experience tremendous tension, anxiety, fear, shame, and embarrassment (W. Bernet, public presentation, May 28, 2011; Warshak, 2010c). Their way of protecting themselves from further experiencing these types of emotions is to adopt one parent's point of view and reject the other parent (W. Bernet, public presentation, May 28, 2011; Warshak, 2010c). Under these circumstances, PAS may not actually be occurring because the children are not being systematically programmed to hate the rejected parent. Nonetheless, many rejected parents believe their child has been alienated by the favored parent (W. Bernet, public presentation, May 28, 2011; Warshak, 2010c). However, it's possible that the child may be experiencing an adjustment disorder with anxiety instead (W. Bernet, public presentation, May 28, 2011).

... When conflict dodging is present, it's extremely important that both parents learn to stop fighting in front of their children and for both parents to encourage their children to have positive relationships with each of them ...

When conflict dodging is present, it's extremely important that both parents learn to stop fighting in front of their children and for both parents to encourage their children to have positive relationships with each of them (W. Bernet, public presentation, May 28, 2011). Dr. Warshak (2010c) also recommends that it's beneficial for both parents to make arrangements to individually drop off and pick up their children where other people are present, such as a school or a community facility, as a way to protect the children from parental combat.

Worry Warts' Inadvertent Programming

Some separated or divorced primary caregivers are constant worry-warts and at times can engage in accidental indoctrination whereby they exhibit a lot of anxiety, tension, worry, and fear that the child picks up on (W. Bernet, public presentation, May 28, 2011). Consequently, the child tends to feel inclined to align with the anxious parent even though the child loves and enjoys being with both parents. This is not parental alienation because neither parent is putting the other parent down in front of the child. A mother may say to her son, for instance, "I'm always worried that you may trip on daddy's front steps of his house because they're so steep. I feel frightened when you're there." However, if this same mother communicates her anxiety to the child and the child ends up fearing and hating the other parent, then the seeds of parental alienation have likely cultivated (W. Bernet, public presentation, May 28, 2011). In either case, professional coaching or counseling is recommended to help the anxious parent gain insight into his or her behaviors as well as to help reduce anxiety (W. Bernet, public presentation, May 28, 2011). The child may also require counseling.

... Some separated or divorced primary caregivers are constant worry-warts and at times can engage in accidental indoctrination whereby they exhibit a lot of anxiety, tension, worry, and fear that the child picks up on ...

As you can probably see, there are some clear reasons why some children refuse to have contact with a parent that don't involve PA or PAS. As well, there are situations such as reversal of the parenting role, accidental indoctrination by anxious parents, and alcohol or substance abuse or dependence that toe the line of parental alienation. No one ever said parenting is an easy job. It's even harder during the separation and divorce process given the myriad of unresolved difficulties that tend to arise. This chapter hopefully serves as a reminder that it's important to take responsibility for your own life and the decisions you make. Ultimately, children pay a high price when a family breakup takes place. I cannot stress enough the importance of seeking help from a qualified mental health professional as soon as possible to obtain an objective evaluation of why contact refusal is occurring. In doing so, it will allow for appropriate treatment interventions to be proposed sooner rather than later. ❧

... Ultimately, children pay a high price when a family breakup takes place. I cannot stress enough the importance of seeking help from a qualified mental health professional as soon as possible to obtain an objective evaluation of why contact refusal is occurring. ...

Time for Self-Reflection

Do you think it's possible that the child in question is engaging in contact refusal for one or more of the above-noted reasons? Or do you believe PA or PAS is actually occurring? Please provide specific reasons why or why not?

_____

_____

_____

_____

_____

_____

_____

_____

_____

_____

_____

_____

What kinds of interventions do you believe are necessary to help the child in question overcome his/her difficulties?

_____

_____

_____

_____

_____

_____

_____

_____

_____

_____

_____

How do you plan to go about this?

_____

_____

_____

_____

_____

_____

_____

_____

_____

Are there other significant things you learned from reading this chapter?

_____

_____

_____

_____

_____

_____

_____

_____

_____

_____

_____

_____

_____

_____

_____

_____

_____

Additional notes:

_____

_____

_____

_____

_____

_____

_____

_____

_____

_____

_____

_____

_____

_____

_____

_____

_____

_____

_____

_____

_____

_____

Chapter Four
What is the Prevalence of PAS?

At this time, we don't know what the exact prevalence of PAS is. Undoubtedly, the phenomenon of PAS will extend to other parts of the world, if it hasn't already. Once it becomes more clearly recognized in each country and the American Psychiatric Association moves to embrace a standardized definition for this mental condition, then it will be much easier to collect official statistics describing the incidence rates globally.

... According to Bernet, Caddy, and Darnall, at the present time there do not appear to be any significant gender differences in who becomes an alienated or target parent. ...

When Gardner initially introduced PAS in the mid 1980s, he argued that as many as 90 percent of children involved in custody litigation demonstrated some symptoms of the syndrome (1998a). At that time, he was seeing more mothers who were programming their children against their fathers than the other way around. As such, he claimed that in nine out of ten cases, the alienated or targeted parent was the father (1998a). This became a source of controversy among critics. Rand (1997a), a forensic psychologist and researcher, found that children were almost twice as likely to develop PAS type alliances with their mothers (1997a). Gardner later changed his position and suggested that the alienated or targeted parent was the father approximately 60 percent of the time in child custody cases (Gardner, 1998b). According to Bernet, Caddy, and Darnall, at the present time there do not appear to be any significant gender differences in who becomes an alienated or target parent. In other words, both fathers and mothers have an equal chance of being alienated (personal communications, May 28, 2011).

Some research studies have been conducted on the prevalence and incidence of PAS (see Baker, 2007a; Bow et al., 2009; Johnston, 1993, 2003, 2005; Kopetski, 1998a, 1998b). All in all, it is estimated that approximately one-quarter million children are exposed to or suffer from PAS each year in the U.S. alone (Warshak, public presentation, February 25, 2011; Warshak & Otis, 2010a). It's heartbreaking because the prevalence of PAS is too often overlooked by the judiciary, mental health professionals, and the media. There are far too many children in society who are suffering from this very real form of abuse and yet have not been identified as experiencing it. Perhaps the primary reason for there being such limited research available on the prevalence and incidence of PAS is because it is extremely difficult to accurately establish the point at which alignment and parental criticism begins (Gardner, 1998b). This is complicated by the fact that there are varying definitions for PA (Bernet, 2010).

It's important to mention that PAS is not just a Canadian and American phenomenon. To date, psychological and legal literature is available in at least thirty countries including the United Kingdom (see Bernet, 2010; Hobbs, 2006), Belgium, Denmark, Finland, Norway, Iceland, the Netherlands, Switzerland, Sweden, France, Italy, Poland, Portugal, Spain, Brazil, South Africa, Argentina, Ukraine, Russia, Czech Republic, Malaysia, Japan, Mexico (see Bernet, 2010), Israel (see Bernet, 2010; Gottlieb, 2006), Germany (see Bernet, 2010; Leitner & Kunneth, 2006), and Australia (see Bernet, 2010; Berns, 2006) on the topic of PAS. In each of the latter countries, no clear-cut statistical findings are provided on the prevalence of PAS. Many mental health professionals worldwide have recognized Gardner's criteria for PAS and have primarily applied his criteria when working with high-conflict divorce cases and other cases involving repeated false allegations of various forms of child abuse or domestic violence (see Bernet, 2010; Gottlier, 2006).

... It's important to mention that PAS is not just a Canadian and American phenomenon. To date, psychological and legal literature is available in at least thirty countries ...

At this time, we don't know the exact prevalence of PAS. Undoubtedly, the phenomenon of PAS will extend to other parts of the world, if it hasn't already. Once it becomes more clearly recognized in each country and the American Psychiatric Association moves to embrace a standardized definition for this mental condition, then it will be much easier to collect official statistics describing the incidence rates globally. ✑

Time for Self-Reflection

List any thoughts and feelings you might have after reading this chapter:

_____

_____

_____

_____

_____

_____

_____

_____

_____

_____

_____

_____

_____

_____

_____

_____

_____

_____

_____

_____

_____

_____

_____

_____

_____

_____

_____

Additional notes:

_____

_____

_____

_____

_____

_____

_____

_____

_____

_____

_____

_____

_____

_____

_____

_____

_____

_____

_____

_____

_____

Chapter Five
Variations in the Severity of PAS

Dr. Richard A. Gardner categorized
three types of PAS in terms of severity—
mild, moderate, or severe. Some of the
eight primary manifestations of PAS are
not revealed in mild or moderate cases of
PAS; however, most, if not all, of the eight
manifestations are revealed in severe cases.

D r. Richard A. Gardner categorized three types of PAS in terms of severity—mild, moderate, or severe. Some of the eight primary manifestations of PAS are not revealed in mild or moderate cases of PAS; however, most, if not all, of the eight manifestations are revealed in severe cases (Gardner, 1992a, 1994, 2006). Gardner's descriptions of each type follow:

...In severe cases of PAS, the child not only fervently abhors the target parent but may also make false allegations of abuse against him or her ...

In mild cases, a certain degree of parental programming is evident, yet it won't gravely disrupt visits between the child and target parent. In moderate cases, however, a considerable degree of parental programming is evident and visits between the child and alienated parent are gravely disrupted. In moderate cases of PAS, the child often experiences difficulties transitioning from one parent's home to the other but tends to settle more readily at the alienating parent's home.

In severe cases of PAS, the child not only fervently abhors the target parent but may also make false allegations of abuse against him or her (Gardner, 1992a, 1994, 2006; Wakefield & Underwager, 1990). Gardner (1994) added that a child's relationship with the target parent might be so detached in serious PAS cases that it is quite difficult to mend.

Darnall (1997; 1998), a clinical psychologist and expert child custody evaluator, agreed with Gardner's postulation that parental alienation consists of three varying degrees of severity. In his attempt to comprehend parental alienation, Darnall derived three alternative classifications regarding the degree of severity—naïve alienation, active alienation, and obsessed alienation. He described them as follows:

> Naïve alienators are parents who are generally passive about the children's relationship with the other parent but will occasionally do or say something to alienate. Active alienators also know better than to alienate, but their intense hurt or anger causes them to impulsively lose control over their behavior or what they say. Later, they may feel guilty about how they behaved.

> Obsessed alienators have a fervent cause: to destroy the target parent. Frequently a parent can be a blend between two types of alienators, usually a combination between the naïve and active alienator. Rarely does the obsessed alienator have enough self-control or insight to blend with the other types (Darnall, 1998, p. 8 - 9).

... Active alienators also know better than to alienate, but their intense hurt or anger causes them to impulsively lose control over their behavior or what they say ...

With regard to empirical evidence on variations in the severity of PAS, thirty court-referred, highly contested custody cases were randomly selected for Burrill's study (2001). Each case was assigned to either the mild, moderate, or severe group based on the parents' symptoms and behaviors as well as the children's symptoms and behaviors, as defined by Gardner's PAS criteria. The results of Burrill's study supported Gardner's clinical observations, conceptualization, and definitions of PAS. Burrill's data analysis revealed that the parents in the severe PAS group had children who demonstrated greater negative behaviors toward the alienated parents compared to the parents in the mild and moderate PAS groups. Moreover, the study's findings suggest that, "the amount of [the children's] negative behaviors and symptoms appears to be directly related to the amount of hostility exhibited by the alienating parent toward the alienated parent" (p. 74).

Recently, Warshak and Otis (2010a) described three other classification types with respect to the variations of this problem—the disillusioned child, the alienated child, and the estranged child. They described them as follows:

The degree of feeling disillusioned or disappointed typically occurs in the early stages of a child becoming alienated. In this stage, the child still spends time with the targeted parent but wants to spend less time with him/her. The child typically blames one parent even though both parents have made mistakes. Some children also may become disillusioned because one of their parents has moved on with his/her life and developed a new relationship with someone else. A new boyfriend or girlfriend, for instance, has entered into the targeted parent's life.

... The degree of feeling disillusioned or disappointed typically occurs in the early stages of a child becoming alienated. In this stage, the child still spends time with the targeted parent but wants to spend less time with him/her ...

The alienated child continues to have contact with the targeted parent but really does not want to. Further, with this degree of severity, the alienated child does not have any nice things to say about the targeted parent, often directing the disparaging comments directly at him/her.

The estranged child is not only alienated but he/she no longer is in contact with the targeted parent. Rather, the estranged child has a close relationship with the alienating or favorite parent. Given the severity, the estranged child believes that the alienating parent is perfect and flawless whereas the targeted parent is all bad.

Carey's (2003) empirical study on the long-term effects of PAS also focused on variations in the severity of PAS. Rather than using Gardner's classification, which reflects "the severity of denigration and ... the severity of the child's disinterest in or refusal to have contact with the target parent" (p. 34), Carey chose to identify the level of alienation by the number of criteria met by the participants. The latter choice was made because her study was retrospective, and it was easier to devise her own measure in a systematic fashion rather than attempt to measure Gardner's classification of the three levels of PAS severity in a systematic fashion.

Based on Gardner's eight manifestations of PAS symptoms, participants in Carey's (2003) study who met three to four out of the eight manifestations were considered to have experienced mild PAS. Participants who met five to six of the eight manifestations were considered to have experienced moderate PAS and those who met seven or eight manifestations were considered to have experienced severe PAS. Of the ten participants in the study, two met some alienation criteria but not enough to be considered mild PAS, three met mild PAS, three met moderate PAS, and two met severe PAS criteria.

As you can see, there are different labels that have been provided for the level of severity in PAS cases. Call me a traditionalist but I choose to use Gardner's three terms—mild, moderate, and severe alienation. To help put his three variations into better perspective, here are some case examples of each type:

... Participants who met five to six of the eight manifestations were considered to have experienced moderate PAS and those who met seven or eight manifestations were considered to have experienced severe PAS...

Jody's Experience of Mild Parental Alienation

Jody, an only child, was fifteen when her parents divorced. She didn't experience tremendous grief, sadness, stress, despair, or surprise at the time. Throughout the years, she was used to her parents yelling and screaming at each other at home and in public. Jody recalls often wishing their marriage would end so she could perhaps experience some peace and quiet.

Jody experienced some feelings of despair after her parents sold their family home. Given her age, Jody's parents let her decide which parent she would live with. Jody chose to reside with her mother. Her father moved into an apartment building approximately six blocks away from them. It became noticeable to Jody that both of her parents were having difficulties coping with the divorce. She spent fairly equal time with each parent. Nonetheless, while Jody was with her mom separately, her mom would spend a great deal of time bad-mouthing her dad. Jody believed her mother and began bad-mouthing him, too.

In grade twelve, Jody started dating another student named Dan. It was love at first sight. They married shortly after graduating from high school. Jody's mother made some of the wedding arrangements really difficult, caused a huge uproar, and refused to sit at the table where Jody's father was sitting. Jody found out that her mother purposefully "forgot" to send wedding invitations to most of her father's side of the family. Additionally, Jody's mother made rude remarks to her ex in front of guests. Fortunately, Jody's father chose not to denigrate his former wife.

Jody has been happily married for nearly three years now. Her mother continues to denigrate her father but Jody has undergone effective therapy. She has managed to ignore her mother's childish behavior.

In this case, only a couple of the characteristics of parental alienation are present. Thus, the alienation Jody has experienced is mild.

Debbie's Experience of Moderate Alienation

... Debbie was seven years old when her parents separated. The oldest child with two younger siblings, she remembers that her mother constantly spoke badly of their father ...

Debbie was seven years old when her parents separated. The oldest child with two younger siblings, she remembers that her mother constantly spoke badly of their father. Her mother said things like he was a bum, a useless twit, and had no time for them. Debbie was told by her mother on numerous occasions that she wanted a divorce but he would not comply. She could not afford an attorney to fight for a divorce because the "bum wasn't giving us any money."

Within six months of the separation, "Uncle Joe", her mom's boyfriend moved in with them. He also began to speak negatively about Debbie's father, saying things like, "Your father and I are completely different. He's a jerk and I'm acting more like a father to you. And don't you forget that I am paying for everything you have. He isn't." All Debbie ever knew about her dad was what her mother and Uncle Joe told her. Subsequently, Debbie refused to hear anything about her father from other people that focused on the good things about him. He sent surprise gifts to her at school in an attempt to have some form of contact. Debbie recalls having no sense of gratitude for them.

The subsequent stages of the alienation process left Debbie and her siblings thinking that the denigration of their father was their own decision. None of them experienced any feelings of guilt. Even though Debbie and her sisters were eventually forced to go to counseling during the divorce process, she recalls saying disrespectful things about him. Debbie knew her father was vulnerable during family counseling sessions so she took advantage of that. Debbie never said anything negative or disrespectful about her mother to the counselor; in fact, Debbie placed her mother on a pedestal.

... Whenever Nathan's father attempted to speak to him over the phone, Nathan's mother came up with a variety of excuses and lies for why it wasn't possible ....

Debbie resented her father for a very long time and did not see him even though her father continued to attempt to have contact with her and her siblings long after the failed marriage and failed counseling attempts. Today, Debbie says her mother is her best friend and they are very close. She maintains a distant relationship with her father, generally having superficial conversations about the weather, sports, or Hollywood happenings.

Nathan's Experience of Moderate to Severe Parental Alienation

Nathan was only two years old when his parents divorced. The court granted his mother sole custody and his father was granted the right to twice monthly weekend visits. Nathan had a very strong attachment to his mother and recalls kicking, screaming, and crying every time he was separated from her. He disliked having to stay at his father's residence for two weekends of each month. Whenever

Nathan's father attempted to speak to him over the phone, Nathan's mother came up with a variety of excuses and lies for why it wasn't possible.

As difficult as it was, Nathan's father was very supportive of him. He paid monthly child support, paid for Nathan's private school tuition from grades one to twelve, paid for his college tuition, and paid for the two of them to go on expensive trips to Disney World, Mexico, and Hawaii during school vacations. And, most of all, his father seemed to be there anytime Nathan needed his emotional needs met. Nathan recalls, however, that the only reason he liked being with his father was to get material things from him. As he grew older, he would fake sickness as a way of not having to see his father, paternal grandparents, and other extended family. Nathan refused to listen to anything about his father especially if it was good.

Nathan acknowledges that he was very spoiled by his mother. She gave him whatever he wanted even though most of her income was the direct result of spousal and child support. After successful alienation by his mother, Nathan gradually created his own denigration of his father. On more than one occasion, Nathan told his teachers and his mother's extended family, "Dad took me to Disney World even though I never wanted to go there."

...His mother provided significant positive reinforcement whenever Nathan told her what was going on in his father's life or how much he despised visiting him. His mother would constantly say, "I don't know how you do it. He's such a jerk. Nothing has changed about him."...

His mother provided significant positive reinforcement whenever Nathan told her what was going on in his father's life or how much he despised visiting him. His mother would constantly say, "I don't know how you do it. He's such a jerk. Nothing has changed about him."

Nathan's mother refused to ever speak to his father. Instead, she would ask others to pass along messages, including teachers, and Nathan. Nathan would often receive cash from his mother as a bribe for keeping secrets from his father. During those times, she would threaten that if he divulged their secret she would force him to move out of her house and he would have no choice but to live with his father or live on the streets. That, of course, was the last thing she and her son wanted.

Currently, Nathan is twenty-two years old and sees his father "once in a while." Nathan is still convinced that his father has never truly loved him, which is the exact opposite of reality.

Shane's Experience of Severe Parental Alienation

Shane was twelve years old when his parents separated and divorced. After the divorce, he and his younger sister lived with their father on the family farm. Their mother could only afford to rent a small bachelor suite and worked two part-time jobs. At the time, she was unable to look after her children and provide adequate space and privacy for the children to stay at the apartment for any lengthy period of time. Shane had a very close relationship with both parents prior to the separation. The divorce came as a surprise because he thought his parents were in love and very happy.

... At first, Shane's father did not attempt to restrict or deny telephone calls or visits by his mother....

At first, Shane's father did not attempt to restrict or deny telephone calls or visits by his mother. Nonetheless, baseball games and other special events took precedence even when they occurred during his mother's scheduled time. But, whenever Shane's mother wanted to spend a little extra time with the children outside of her scheduled times, the father prevented it. Interestingly enough, Shane believed that because he was primarily living with his father and was mainly around him, that his father was always telling the truth about his mother. Shane, therefore, agreed that his mother was unreliable and very selfish, among many other things.

After going back and forth between the two family homes for approximately seven months, Shane began to have increased negative perceptions about his mother. She seemed really exhausted, and grumpy. He would describe his mother's behaviors to his father upon returning to the farm. Shane's father validated his thoughts and feelings, saying, "Your mother was always a tired grump. That's one of the reasons I couldn't take it anymore. Now you know what I had to put up with all those years."

Shane's father encouraged him not to bother visiting the grump anymore. It was considered a waste of valuable time. Shane told his friends, teachers, and others that he independently refused to see her. Shane truly believed that his mother was a bad mother. He began to feel sorry for his father for being left on his own to raise two young teens. Even though his mother continued to send gifts for birthdays, Christmas, and other special occasions, Shane believed it was purely because she must have felt guilty. Shane borrowed his father's expression and referred to the gifts as "guilt offerings" because she never helped out financially. At school, Shane had no problem telling his friends and teachers about the guilt offerings.

As time passed, Shane refused to have anything to do with his mother. He never felt guilty because he thought she deserved it. Sadly, Shane's mother died of terminal cancer six years later. Shane didn't attend her funeral. As far as he was concerned, she deserved to die. Plus, he wanted nothing to do with his maternal grandparents who attended the "bitch's" funeral. Shane was manipulated so badly by his father in earlier years, and with the constant brainwashing, Shane had only resentment and hatred toward his mother.

Throughout adolescence, Shane was taught by his father not to trust women. Today, Shane is in his mid twenties and has difficulties with commitment and trusting women; he's been married and divorced twice to date. He moved back to the farm to live with his aging father. Additionally, Shane was recently diagnosed with severe depression and Ewing's Sarcoma, a type of bone cancer. ✍

... Shane truly believed that his mother was a bad mother. He began to feel sorry for his father for being left on his own to raise two young teens. Even though his mother continued to send gifts for birthdays, Christmas, and other special occasions, Shane believed it was purely because she must have felt guilty ...

Time for Self-Reflection

Write down whether you believe your family or someone else's that you are reading this book about is experiencing mild, moderate, or severe variations of PAS. List all the reasons why:

Note: In some cases, there will be an overlap of mild to moderate variations of PAS just as there can be an overlap of moderate to severe variations of PAS.

_____

_____

_____

_____

_____

_____

_____

_____

_____

_____

_____

_____

_____

_____

_____

_____

_____

_____

_____

_____

_____

_____

_____

Additional notes:

_____

_____

_____

_____

_____

_____

_____

_____

_____

_____

_____

_____

_____

_____

_____

_____

_____

_____

_____

Chapter Six
Long-Term Effects of PAS

PAS is a significant form of abuse and some research studies have consistently shown that children and youth who have been subject to PAS also experience psychological difficulties in their adult years.

The Brody longitudinal study[1] explored the emotional development of seventy-six participants from varying socioeconomic backgrounds from birth to age thirty (Massie & Szajnberg, 2004). Although this particular study did not focus on the long-term outcomes of PAS, it did reveal that parental abuse (physical, verbal, and emotional abuse and neglect) clearly damages children. By age thirty, many of the participants who had been maltreated from infancy to age eighteen suffered from various problems such as chronic depression, dysthymia, substance abuse, anxiety disorders, personality disorders, and various physical complaints.

...By age thirty, many of the participants who had been maltreated from infancy to age eighteen suffered from various problems such as chronic depression, dysthymia, substance abuse, anxiety disorders, personality disorders, and various physical complaints ...

PAS is a significant form of abuse and some research studies have consistently shown that children and youth who have been subject to PAS also experience similar psychological difficulties in their adult years, as found in the Brody longitudinal study, as well as some other difficulties. Let's take a look at some research that has been conducted on the long-term effects of PAS.

Carey's (2003) published dissertation incorporated a mixed study on the long-term effects of PAS. She gathered quantitative data on the participants' demographics and gathered qualitative data by

[1] In a longitudinal study, a single group of people is followed over the course of several months or years, and data related to the characteristic(s) under investigation are collected at various times.

conducting extensive, in-depth interviews of ten participants (ages eighteen to thirty-one) to determine the meaning and impact of parental alienation. Her research study mainly focused on the nature of relationships between alienating parents and children as well as between alienated parents and children. All of the participants in Carey's study underwent some dynamics of alienation that significantly influenced their adult development, in particular the ability to have healthy romantic relationships. Many of the study participants still held their negative beliefs about their alienated parents, and many had not resolved their differences or reunited with their alienated parents.

Raso's (2004) published thesis also explored long-term consequences of PAS and found some similar findings as Carey. Many of the participants in Raso's qualitative retrospective study experienced commitment issues throughout adolescence and adulthood; numerous participants chose not to marry. Similar to Carey's findings, Raso found that the majority of participants who experienced severe PAS in childhood had not resolved or reestablished a relationship with their alienated parents. Further outcomes in Raso's study indicated that many participants who experienced severe alienation in childhood held nontraditional views of marriage. Most of them desired to live in open marriages and have multiple sexual partners rather than live in monogamous relationships. Sixty-seven percent of the participants who had married eventually divorced. The majority of participants in Raso's study also experienced significant trust issues with other individuals who shared the same gender as their alienated parents.

... All of the participants in Carey's study underwent some dynamics of alienation that significantly influenced their adult development, in particular the ability to have healthy romantic relationships ...

Baker (2005a) conducted a qualitative retrospective study on the long-term outcomes of PA on a small sample of thirty-eight adults (twenty-four females and fourteen males between nineteen and sixty-seven years old). Her study revealed that a significant number of participants experienced trust issues (in self and others), low self-esteem, depression, substance abuse problems, as well as divorce and alienation from their own offspring. Approximately one year later, Baker (2006) carried out a qualitative retrospective study on the long-term implications of PAS on a sample of forty adults (twenty-five females and fifteen males between nineteen and sixty-seven years old) who experienced PAS in earlier years. There were six significant findings.

First, Baker found that parental alienation does not occur exclusively in separated and divorced families; it can also take place in intact families. Second, in the cases studied, most of the alienating parents were perceived to have engaged in child maltreatment, suffered from alcoholism, and personality disorders. Third, not all participants who experienced alienation in childhood had been involved in post-divorce litigation. Fourth, some of the alienated parents may have contributed to their own alienation. Fifth, many participants had not wholeheartedly internalized the alienation; rather, many of the participants experienced a combination of ambivalent negative feelings and positive feelings toward the alienated parent throughout their lives. Lastly, three specific types of parental alienation were identified: (a) narcissistic alienating mothers in intact families, (b) narcissistic alienating mothers in divorced families, and (c) abusive or rejecting alienating mothers and fathers.

In 2007, I conducted a quantitative research study to examine the long-term effects of PAS. One hundred and fifty individuals between the ages of eighteen and thirty-five living in the Okanagan Region of British Columbia, Canada, who experienced divorce in earlier years, and who met other selection criteria participated in the study. The research question was: Do adult children of divorce with different levels of PAS show corresponding levels of psychological distress as measured by the Symptom Assessment-45 Questionnaire (SA-45) (Strategic Advantage, Inc., 2003).

... Baker found that parental alienation does not occur exclusively in separated and divorced families, rather, it can also take place in intact families ...

There was one testable hypothesis. The independent variable was adult children of divorce scores on the Parental Alienation Syndrome Questionnaire (PASQ) (Machuca, 2005) consisting of five levels: never, minimally, occasionally, often, most of the time. Two separate PASQ instruments were given to the participants. One determined whether or not the mother might have inflicted alienation during or after the divorce along with contributions from the participant. The other determined whether or not the father might have inflicted alienation during or after the divorce along with contributions from the participant.

The dependent variable was the level of psychological distress. The total score on the Symptom Assessment-45 Questionnaire (SA-45) (Strategic Advantage, Inc., 2003) was used to assess current psychological distress. The study's findings demonstrated that adult children of divorce who perceived experiencing greater levels of PAS also perceived experiencing greater levels of psychological distress such as depression, anxiety, hostility, interpersonal sensitivity, obsessive compulsivity, paranoid ideation, phobic anxiety, hallucinations, delusions, and the presence of certain physical symptoms such as feelings of numbness, soreness, tingling, and heaviness in various parts of the body.

... most researchers agree that targeted parents and their alienated children, primarily in severe PAS cases, are less likely to reestablish a bond later in life ...

To date, most researchers agree that targeted parents and their alienated children, primarily in severe PAS cases, are less likely to reestablish a bond later in life (Cartwright, 1993; Ellis, 2000; Gardner, 1998a, Stahl, 1999; Vassiliou, 2001). Of course, this is especially the case when the alienated child refuses to have contact with the targeted parent and the targeted parent continues to respect the child's wishes (Gardner, 1998a). According to Gardner, "After many years of little if any contact, the whole foundation of the relationship becomes eroded. The common experiences that serve as the fundamental building blocks of the relationship have become eroded to the point of nonexistence" (1998a, p. 362).

Please keep in mind that some children, youths, and adult-children do change their minds. Some, for instance, eventually acknowledge that they have been programmed by an alienating parent. Following is a brief story of a 32-year-old woman who sent her mother an email out of the blue after being severely alienated and estranged for over twenty years.

Hi mom. I'm sorry it's been such a long time since we've touched base. I've been doing my best to picture the perfect scenario of how I would reconnect with you. For months, I've been thinking how should I do this? Where do I start? What will happen when I send you this email? Will you care? Will you respond? Will you be angry? Will we be able to repair our relationship or is it too late and you've moved on? I've made countless half attempts at writing you an email. Both of us are getting older and I really don't want to lose any more time. I'm hoping that you will be a part of my life again. I am so sorry that I shut you out of my life. I now have my head on straight and realize that you were an amazing mother and did so much for me. For various reasons, I obviously wasn't able to see these things back then. I do see them now and nothing would mean more to me than connecting with you again. I hope you will feel okay about replying to this email. I truly miss you and want to connect with you again. Please contact me.

... For those of you who are wounded sufferers of toxic divorce and are desperately waiting to hear from your estranged child no matter how much time has elapsed, it's my hope that you will be able to take some comfort in knowing that anything is possible ...

Fortunately, this particular mother and daughter have reconciled their relationship. For those of you who are wounded sufferers of toxic divorce and are desperately waiting to hear from your estranged child no matter how much time has elapsed, it's my hope that you will be able to take some comfort in knowing that anything is possible. There is reason for hope and optimism. Hopefully, alienated children who have the opportunity to read this book will recognize themselves in it and have the courage to take the first step in rekindling their relationship with their alienated parent. Truly, there is nothing in the world that could be more important than restoring your relationship with your mom or dad. ∞

Time for Self-Reflection

List all your concerns about the potential long-term effects of PAS about the alienated child in question. Please be specific:

_____

_____

_____

_____

_____

_____

_____

_____

_____

_____

_____

_____

_____

_____

_____

_____

_____

_____

_____

_____

_____

_____

_____

_____

_____

_____

_____

Additional notes:

_____

_____

_____

_____

_____

_____

_____

_____

_____

_____

_____

_____

_____

_____

_____

_____

_____

_____

_____

_____

Chapter Seven
Psychological Characteristics of Alienated Children

It appears that certain psychological characteristics will make children more vulnerable to the fallout of alienation ...

A 1985 study conducted by Johnston, Campbell, and Mayers found that children between six and twelve years of age will typically behave in disturbing manners during parental conflict. For example, children will demonstrate anxiety, tension, depression, and psychosomatic illness. In PAS cases, however, children appear to suffer far more consequences. Cartwright (1993) pointed out that alienated children will initially experience the loss of the targeted parent as well as the continued barrage of denigration against the targeted parent and his or her extended family. Years after, these same children tend to develop guilty feelings (Cartwright, 1993).

... It appears that certain psychological characteristics will make children more vulnerable to the fallout of alienation ...

It appears that certain psychological characteristics will make children more vulnerable to the fallout of alienation. Stahl's (1999) literature suggested that those who are most susceptible in alienation situations tend to have passive and dependent tendencies. Given that alienated children are caught in a battle between parents, it's difficult for them to maintain healthy relationships and boundaries. Consequently, these children generally feel a strong need and desire to psychologically care for the alienating parent (Stahl, 1999).

Dunne and Hedrick (1994, p. 9) added, "Children are apt to be susceptible to alienation when they perceive the alienating parent's emotional survival or the survival of their relationship with the alienating parent is dependent on the child's rejection of the other parent." According to Johnston and Roseby (1997), when a child perceives that the alienating parent is in a precarious emotional state, then he or she may want to play the roles of caregiver and protector for the alienator. In many instances, the alienating parent is the primary caregiver of the alienated child; therefore, he or she is the only adult whom the child can trust to meet his or her own needs (Johnston & Roseby, 1997). Accordingly, children may be motivated to do whatever it takes to protect their relationship with the alienating parent, even if that means rejecting the target parent (Dunne & Hedrick, 1994; Gardner, 1994; Johnston & Roseby, 1997).

Gardner (1998a) believed that severe types of PAS typically halt the ability for alienated children to have a same-sex role model or an opposite-sex role model. Consequently, alienated children may have relationship difficulties with non-familial individuals who are of the same or opposite sex. Gardner also argued that alienated children may have a distorted sense of reality due to PAS because they are programmed to believe that things do not coincide with their observations and experiences. This can produce confusion, feelings of self-doubt, low self-worth, distrust of those who tell them things different from the programmer, and in extreme cases, psychotic breaks with reality (Gardner, 1998a, p. 364).

... children may be motivated to do whatever it takes to protect their relationship with the alienating parent, even if that means rejecting the target parent ...

Overall, children who are victims of PAS tend to exhibit a variety of behaviors and symptoms. These include the following: disconnections in their relationships, clinging and separation anxiety, difficulties in forming intimate relationships, an inability to tolerate anger or hostility in other relationships, conflicts with authority figures, impulse control issues, developing fears and phobias, anxiety and panic attacks, obsessive-compulsive behaviors, and a lack of self-confidence and self-esteem (Lowenstein, 2006; Stahl, 1999). Additionally, PAS children tend to reveal psychosomatic symptoms, depression and suicidal ideation, sleep or eating disorders, psychological vulnerability and dependency, involuntary bodily functions such as bedwetting, educational difficulties, damaged sexual identity, drug abuse and self-destructive behaviors, poor peer relationships, excessive guilty feelings, and an unhealthy sense of entitlement for one's age that leads to social alienation in general (Lowenstein, 2006; Stahl, 1999).

Gardner (2002a) provided some DSM-IV diagnoses applicable to alienated children. One diagnosis that may be warranted for both the alienating parent and the PAS child is shared psychotic disorder (Gardner, 2002a). (More will be discussed about shared psychotic disorder in chapter 9.) Other diagnoses that may be applicable to PAS children are conduct disorder, separation anxiety disorder, dissociative disorder not otherwise specified, adjustment disorders, and disorder of infancy, childhood, or adolescence not otherwise specified (Gardner, 2002a).

... There is one thing that I can assure you about alienated children: all alienated children see things in absolute black and white categories with respect to their parents ...

There is one thing that I can assure you about alienated children: all alienated children see things in absolute black and white categories with respect to their parents. One parent is all good, superior, outstanding, preferential, and faultless whereas the other parent is all bad, substandard, un-stupendous, rejected, and utterly full of faults. The alienated child experiences significant irrational perceptions about both parents. They have no positive perceptions of the alienated parent just as they have no negative perceptions of the alienating parent.

You may find it interesting to know that alienated children absolutely refuse to listen to anyone including mental health professionals, teachers, school principals, clergy members, friends, extended family members, and the targeted parent who may attempt to share any rational, objective evidence about the alienated parent. It has been my experience in clinical settings that when attempts are made, the alienated child will say things like: "He has never been like that." "Well, you really don't know her like I do." "If that's what you think about him, then you're way wrong. He's not like that at all." Or, "She's fooling you, if that's what you think."

Research conducted by Dr. John Gottman at the University of Washington in Seattle found that there are four attitudes that highly predict the dissolution of a relationship. They are: 1) criticism, 2) contempt, 3) defensiveness, and 4) stonewalling, especially when combined with each other (Gottman & Silver, 1999).

Criticism refers to shaming and attacking your partner's character or personality, usually with the intent of making someone right and someone wrong.

Examples are:

- *"You always ...."*

- *"You never ...."*

- *"Why are you such a ...."*

- *"You're just the kind of person who ...."*

> *... there are four attitudes that highly predict the dissolution of a relationship. They are: 1) criticism, 2) contempt, 3) defensiveness, and 4) stonewalling, especially when combined with each other ...*

Contempt refers to attacking your partner's sense of self with the intention to insult or mentally abuse him/her.

Examples are:

- Name calling or hurling insults such as *"You are: lazy, fat, ugly, a slob, a bitch, a bastard."*

- Engaging in mockery, sarcasm, or bad humor or showing certain negative body gestures such as curling your upper lip, rolling your eyes, and frowning.

Defensiveness refers to seeing oneself as a victim and having the need to defend or protect him/herself whenever perceiving attack from the other partner.

Examples are:

- Using *"yes, but"* statements.

- Making up excuses such as, *"It is not my fault what happened."*

- Ignoring what the other partner says.

- You may link your partner's complaint or criticism with a complaint or criticism of your own.

- Whining such as, *"It's not fair that ...."*

- You may disagree with your partner, then cross-complain with phrases such as, *"That is absolutely not true. You are the one who...."*

- Or you may repeat yourself several times and ignore what your partner is saying.

... after studying more than 2,000 married couples over a period of twenty years, Gottman noticed significant patterns about how partners relate to each other, which can be used to predict with 94 percent accuracy which marriages will succeed and which marriages will fail ...

Stonewalling refers to withdrawing and pulling away from the relationship in an attempt to avoid conflict in the relationship. Even though the stonewalling partner may believe he/she is trying to be neutral, his/her stonewalling behaviors convey the message of distance, separation, disconnection, and disapproval.

Examples are:

- Being smug.

- Having a silent temper tantrum.

• Muttering things.

• Physically removing yourself from your partner.

Interestingly, after studying more than 2,000 married couples over a period of twenty years, Gottman noticed significant patterns about how partners relate to each other, which can be used to predict with 94 percent accuracy which marriages will succeed and which marriages will fail.

Although no scientific research has been conducted to date utilizing Gottman's four attitudes that highly predict the dissolution of a relationship involving PA and PAS cases, my hypothesis based on numerous clinical experiences with alienated families is that alienated children, dependent on the level of severity of alienation being experienced—mild, moderate, or severe—also engage in criticism, contempt, defensiveness, and stonewalling much in the same manner as defined by Gottman's research. ✎

... alienated children, dependent on the level of severity of alienation being experienced— mild, moderate, or severe— also engage in criticism, contempt, defensiveness, and stone- walling ...

Time for Self-Reflection

List some current behaviors and symptoms that the alienated child in question is exhibiting at present:

_____

_____

_____

_____

_____

_____

_____

_____

_____

_____

_____

How does that really make you feel?

_____

_____

_____

_____

_____

_____

_____

_____

_____

_____

_____

_____

_____

_____

In your opinion, how have those behaviors changed in the alienated child in question since you recognized that PA or PAS is likely occurring?

_____
_____
_____
_____
_____
_____
_____
_____
_____
_____
_____
_____

And, how does that really make you feel?

_____
_____
_____
_____
_____
_____
_____
_____
_____
_____
_____
_____
_____
_____
_____
_____

Additional notes:

_____

_____

_____

_____

_____

_____

_____

_____

_____

_____

_____

_____

_____

_____

_____

_____

_____

_____

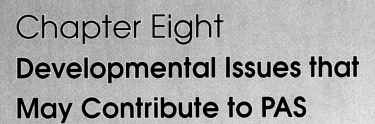

Chapter Eight
Developmental Issues that
May Contribute to PAS

*Children caught in the middle of toxic divorce cases,
dependent on their age range, align differently with
the alienating parent...*

Johnston (1993) explored PAS from a developmental perspective and found that children caught in the middle of toxic divorce cases, dependent on their age range, align differently with the alienating parent as follows:

Two to three years old: Children between two and three years of age typically demonstrate age-appropriate separation anxiety from the parent. However, their anxiety will increase when the primary parent shows emotional disturbance.

Three to six years old: Children between three and six years of age will typically shift their alignments according to which parent they are with at the time. At this age range, children have not developed the capacity to comprehend two varying points of view. Consequently, three to six year olds do not have the ability to comprehend why one parent will say one thing while the other parent says another thing.

Six to seven years old: Children between six and seven years of age typically are sensitive to hurting their parents. Typically, they will experience conflicting loyalties between one parent and the other.

Seven to nine years old: Children between seven and nine years of age typically have the ability to comprehend each parent's perspectives as well as understand how one perspective may be conflictual with the other.

... children caught in the middle of toxic divorce cases, dependent on their age range, align differently with the alienating parent ...

Nine to twelve years old: Children between nine and twelve years of age typically are the most vulnerable to PAS primarily because they are old enough to have established a strong alignment with one parent. In this age range, children have the ability to try to resolve loyalty conflicts by picking one parent over the other.

Twelve to seventeen years old: Youths between twelve and seventeen years of age typically continue to align with one parent over the other in PAS cases. Although most youths have the ability to take a more mature and independent view of their parents' arguments, a significant proportion will uphold their alignment and continue to reject one parent in favor of the other parent (Johnston, 1993). ❧

...Youths between twelve and seventeen years of age typically continue to align with one parent over the other in PAS cases...

Time for Self-Reflection

Does the alienated child in question align with the alienating parent based on their developmental age range as outlined above? What are the similarities and differences? Do you notice any overlap between some age categories?

_____

_____

_____

_____

_____

_____

_____

_____

_____

_____

_____

_____

_____

_____

_____

_____

_____

_____

_____

_____

_____

_____

Chapter Nine
Psychological Characteristics of Alienating Parents

Alienating parents are indisputably troubled individuals who look and often act normal, thus, making it difficult for the judiciary and the general public to be aware of their chaotic patterns of thinking, feeling, and behaving or interacting.

Alienating parents are indisputably troubled individuals who look and often act normal, thus, making it difficult for the judiciary and the general public to be aware of their chaotic patterns of thinking, feeling, and behaving or interacting. What alienating parents do to their children, the other parent, and society at large is astounding.

... What alienating parents do to their children, the other parent, and society at large is astounding ...

Gardner (1994) described alienating parents as hostile, defensive, lacking insight, and projecting blame onto others. Other experts believe that alienating parents employ denial to cope with emotional pain, are overly suspicious and distrustful, lack an ability to be intimate with partners, and experience anxiety or self-insight difficulties (Garrity & Baris, 1994). Major (2000) found that alienating parents do not have the ability to individuate; therefore, they cannot perceive their children as separate entities from themselves. Enmeshment (over-involvement) with their children is common (Major, 2000). Johnston and Roseby (1997) found that some alienating parents look to their children for guidance and friendship; many alienators use permissive parenting styles.

Various literature suggests that a frequent motive for the development of PAS is a desire for revenge (Clawar & Rivlin, 1991; Ellis, 2000; Gardner, 1998a; Rand, 1997a). Accordingly, some parents may alienate a child in an attempt to retaliate against the target parent. Some may focus on the target parent's alleged problems as an attempt to deflect attention from their own problems with alcohol, drugs, abusive and neglectful parenting (Clawar & Rivlin, 1991; Ellis, 2000; Gardner, 1998a; Rand, 1997a).

A recent qualitative study found that adult children's descriptions of alienating parents were very similar to the way cult leaders are described by ex-cult members (Baker, 2005b; Baker, 2007b). Alienating parents were described as using "many of the same emotional manipulation and persuasion techniques cult leaders use to heighten dependency on them" (Baker, 2005b, p. 1). Moreover, "the alienating parents seemed to benefit from the alienation much the way cult leaders benefit from the cult: they have excessive control, power, and adulation" (Baker, 2005b, p. 1).

Although rare, some alienators have been diagnosed with Muchausen Syndrome, a type of mental illness in which a person repeatedly acts as if he or she has a physical or mental disorder when, in truth, he or she has caused the symptoms (Andritzky, 2006). It's a type of factitious disorder.

> *... Although rare, some alienators have been diagnosed with Muchausen Syndrome, a type of mental illness in which a person repeatedly acts as if he or she has a physical or mental disorder when, in truth, he or she has caused the symptoms ...*

Although relatively uncommon, some alienators have been diagnosed with delusional disorders (Andritzky, 2006; Rand, 1997a). The essential feature of the delusional disorder is the presence of a persistent, nonbizarre delusion that is not due to any other mental disorder (American Psychiatric Association, 1994). Delusional disorders amongst alienators tend to involve one or more systematic and circumscribed delusions often of a persecutory nature (Gardner, 2002a). For instance, the alienator may believe that he or she is being malevolently treated or deceived by their ex when in fact, it's the other way around.

As mentioned, in one of his many publications, Gardner (2002a) wrote about another diagnosis that may be applicable to alienating parents and their alienated children called shared psychotic disorder (meaning that the diagnosis may be applicable to both the alienating parent and the PAS child). This type of psychotic disorder is rare; when it occurs, the child begins believing the delusions of the alienating parent.

Gardner (1992a) reported that parents who make false allegations of child abuse, conceivably those who fit the severe type of parental alienation, are likely to demonstrate characteristics of various personality disorders, which will be described in detail below. Similar to Gardner's findings, Wakefield and Underwager's (1990) research on false allegations made by one parent against another in child custody battles found that alienating parents tend to be diagnosed with personality disorders compared to parents who do not make such allegations.

Siegel and Langford (1998) conducted a study whereby they compared one group of parents who engaged in PAS (using Gardner's eight manifestations of symptoms) during child custody proceedings to those who did not. They utilized the Minnesota Multiphasic Personality Inventory, revised second edition (MMPI-2), which is a psychological test that is widely used in child custody and other court cases. It provides clear, valid descriptions of people's problems, symptoms, and characteristics. The results of their study confirmed that PAS parents compared to non-PAS parents deliberately tried to present themselves in a very favorable way. In other words, they tried to present themselves as being perfect and not having any kind of emotional problems. Given that the PAS parents answered the test items in a more defensive manner than other parents in child custody cases suggests that many PAS parents have certain types of personality disorders.

What are Personality Disorders?

Personality disorders cause enduring patterns of inner experience and behavior that deviate from the expectations of society. Personality disorders are pervasive, inflexible and stable

...parents who make false allegations of child abuse, conceivably those who fit the severe type of parental alienation, are likely to demonstrate characteristics of various personality disorders ...

over time, and lead to significant distress or impairment in the individual. Specific situations or events can trigger the behaviors of a personality disorder. Some deviations may be quite mild and interfere very little with the person's home or work life whereas others may cause great disruption in both the family and society. Although it's not impossible, it is very difficult to provide treatment to those with personality disorders because they have difficulty getting along with others including physicians and mental health professionals. Additionally, most with personality disorders choose not to seek treatment and those who do often drop out of individual or group counseling sessions prematurely.

The onset of personality disorders tends to occur during adolescence or in early adulthood (American Psychiatric Association, 1994). A recent National U.S. survey reports that approximately 9 percent of U.S. adults have a personality disorder, many of whom also experience other co-existing mental disorders (Lenzenweger, Lane, Loranger & Kessler, 2007). The most common types of personality disorders seen in some alienating parents are 1) borderline personality disorder; 2) histrionic personality disorder; 3) narcissistic personality disorder; 4) paranoid personality disorder; and 5) antisocial personality disorder. A brief description of each type follows:

...Although it's not impossible, it is very difficult to provide treatment to those with personality disorders because they have difficulty getting along with others including physicians and mental health professionals...

Borderline Personality Disorder

Persons with borderline personalities exhibit diverse combinations of anger, anxiety, and intense and rapid changes in emotions. They tend to experience brief disturbances of consciousness such as depersonalization and dissociation. They also present with chronic loneliness, a sense of emptiness, boredom, volatile interpersonal relations, identity confusion, and impulsive behavior that can include physically self-damaging acts like suicidal gestures, self-mutilation including cutting behaviors, or the provocation of fights.

Persons with this type of personality disorder fluctuate quickly between idealizing and clinging to another individual to devaluing and opposing that individual. They are extremely rejection-sensitive and experience abandonment and depression following the slightest of stressors. Thus, interpersonal relationships develop very quickly and intensely, yet tend to be superficial. They are inclined to see others as all good or all bad. They have great difficulty reasoning logically and learning from past experiences and relationships. They tend to blame others when things go wrong (American Psychiatric Association, 1994).

Histrionic Personality Disorder

Persons with histrionic personalities tend to initially seem charming, likable, dramatic, expressive, energetic, and seductive. Over time, however, they are likely to be seen as emotionally unstable, egocentric, and very immature. They tend to be demanding, self-indulgent, and inconsiderate. With others, they also tend to be exhibitionistic and flirtatious, with attention-seeking and manipulativeness being prominent. Those with histrionic personality disorders are unlikely to be analytical thinkers. It's very common for histrionic individuals to experience emotional outbursts. Similar to those with borderline personality disorders, these individuals are also exceedingly rejection-sensitive (American Psychiatric Association, 1994).

... Persons with histrionic personalities tend to initially seem charming, likable, dramatic, expressive, energetic, and seductive ...

Narcissistic Personality Disorder

Individuals with narcissistic personality disorder generally are conceited, boastful, snobbish, self-assured, self-centered, pompous, impatient, and arrogant. They tend to be exploitative, irresponsible, lack empathy, use others to indulge themselves, and are disdainful. They have illusions of specialness and entitlement. They fantasize about having unlimited success, power, beauty, ideal love, and brilliance. Not only do they expect excessive admiration and preferential treatment, but they also expect to associate with other special, unique, or high-status individuals or belong to prestigious organizations (American Psychiatric Association, 1994).

Paranoid Personality Disorder

Persons with paranoid personalities come across as aloof, emotionally cold, humorless, unjustifiably suspicious, hypersensitive, jealous, and are fearful of intimacy. They can be grandiose, contentious, rigid, and litigious. They tend to project blame on others and are very hypersensitive to criticism. Often, they lead isolated lives and are disliked by other people. They also tend to be guarded, defensive, argumentative, and secretive. They scrutinize every situation encountered and look for clues or evidence to confirm their preconceptions rather than objectively focus on facts. They tend to disregard evidence that does not fit their preconceptions. Under stressful circumstances, their thinking can take on a conspiratorial or even delusional twist (American Psychiatric Association, 1994).

... Persons with paranoid personalities come across as aloof, emotionally cold, humorless, unjustifiably suspicious, hypersensitive, jealous, and are fearful of intimacy ....

Antisocial Personality Disorder

Antisocial personality disorder is sometimes known as sociopathic personality disorder. A sociopath is a particularly severe form of antisocial personality disorder. Martha Stout, a Harvard Clinical Psychologist, wrote a fascinating book called *The Sociopath Next Door*. In it, she states that one in twenty-five people are sociopaths. According to the DSM-IV diagnostic criteria, the behavioral style of antisocial personalities is characterized by irresponsible parenting, poor job performance, repeated substance abuse, persistent lying, delinquency, truancy, and violations of others' rights. These individuals also demonstrate impulsive anger, hostility, and cunningness. They frequently engage in risk-seeking and thrill-seeking behaviors and are forceful, antagonistic, and belligerent. They are poor losers, highly competitive, and distrustful of others. At times, they appear to be slick and calculating. They easily rationalize their own behaviors because they are contemptuous of authority, rules, and social expectations. Their emotions are best characterized as being shallow, superficial, non-empathic, and callous toward the pain and suffering of others. They show little if any guilt or shame for their own deviant actions. They have no moral conscience. These individuals fail at work, change jobs frequently, tend to receive dishonorable discharges from the military, are abusing parents, and neglectful spouses. They have grave difficulty maintaining intimate relationships and many are often convicted of various criminal activities and make up a significant percentage of the prison population (American Psychiatric Association, 1994). ⌁

A Note to Readers:

... only qualified clinicians in psychiatry and clinical/forensic psychology can ethically and legally conduct proper assessments and make a proper diagnosis ...

It has been my experience that a significant number of alienated parents are rather quick at assuming and diagnosing their ex with a personality disorder. The fact is that personality disorders really exist. However, only qualified clinicians in psychiatry and clinical/forensic psychology can ethically and legally conduct proper assessments and make a proper diagnosis. For instance, an individual may demonstrate a borderline personality style but not have borderline personality disorder. Moreover, there are a host of other reasons why an alienating parent may be acting the way he or she does. The bottom line is, please don't jump to conclusions about an alienating parent's characteristics or behaviors without proper consultation with a competent mental health professional. These types of accusations are harmful and inappropriate.

Time for Self-Reflection

List the various behaviors and personality traits that the alienating parent in your situation is exhibiting. Explore the similarities and differences from what you read above:

_____

_____

_____

_____

_____

_____

_____

_____

_____

_____

_____

Do you believe that the alienating parent in your situation has a desire for revenge? If so, what evidence supports this?

_____

_____

_____

_____

_____

_____

_____

_____

_____

_____

Do you have any concerns that the alienating parent in your situation may be suffering from a type of personality disorder? If so, what evidence do you have?

_____

_____

_____

_____

_____

_____

_____

_____

_____

_____

_____

Additional Notes:

_____

_____

_____

_____

_____

_____

_____

_____

_____

_____

_____

PART TWO

*Children are natural mimics who act
like their parents despite every effort
to teach them good manners.*

Author Unknown

Chapter Ten
An Emotional Roller Coaster Ride

This chapter contains lists of the types of emotions (feelings) that alienated parents generally experience.

This chapter contains lists of the types of emotions (feelings) that alienated parents generally experience. Although the lists that follow are quite extensive, please keep in mind that there are numerous other feelings that an alienated parent may undergo that are not listed here. I cannot stress enough how important it is to become acquainted with the types of emotions listed in this chapter if you are being alienated. Unfortunately, but true, you will experience an incredible emotional roller coaster ride for an undetermined period of time dependent on numerous factors. There will be no such thing as a flat-line. In other words, you will undoubtedly and expectedly experience a wide array of emotions hourly, daily, weekly, monthly, or perhaps even for years to come. As a matter of fact, don't be surprised to find out that there may be a great deal of the English language that is in your vernacular!

Whatever you do, please don't try to dismiss, deny or repress your feelings. Do not postpone your emotional pain. Give yourself permission to feel what you feel. It's okay to feel what you feel. Process it. It's not okay to hide your feelings from yourself or others. It will not go away even if you attempt to repress it. It's not healthy for you. In actuality, delayed pain will become more painful for you. The honest truth is you must deal with it now or it will create further problems for you including, but not limited to, the following possibilities:

- Depression

- Suicidal thoughts or attempts

- Anxiety

- Paranoia

- Fear

- Guilt

- Anger

- Mood altering addictive behaviors including overworking; problem gambling; compulsive shopping; compulsive over-spending; smoking; disordered eating; relationship, codependency and/or sexual addictions

- Mind altering addictive behaviors including alcohol and drug use, abuse, and dependence

... Keep in mind that resolving your pain will eventually lead to the ability to move on with your life no matter what happens ...

The above-noted self-destructive problems may deaden your pain temporarily but your feelings must be expressed and felt constructively. You don't need to suffer alone. None of us can pretend we are Superman or Superwoman for very long. Therefore, I urge you to please make a diligent effort to feel the pain, express it, share it, and eventually grow from it. Your growth will take place because you have experienced the pain rather than giving in to the urge to delay processing it.

Keep in mind that resolving your pain will eventually lead to the ability to move on with your life no matter what happens. Even though your emotional pain will never be entirely forgotten, it will eventually decrease and even likely cease. At any time you can decide to move out of the cycle of destruction due to the ramifications of PAS and move into the process of recovery from PAS.

If you happen to be a family member, friend, acquaintance, or professional reading this chapter and you know an alienated parent and want to support him or her, then it is also very important that you become acquainted with the numerous types of emotions experienced during the alienation process. In doing so, you will have a wonderful gift to give them; you will have the ability to communicate to them what you imagine they are feeling. Active listening skills, thought empathy, and feelings empathy go such a long way. The alienated individual will likely feel validated and supported by you.

The rest of the chapter provides three different lists of typical emotions experienced by alienated parents. The first list is typical anxiety-related emotions, the second list is typical mood-related emotions, and the third list is typical anger-related emotions of an alienated parent. Feel free to use a pencil or pen and circle the ones you tend to identify with. In chapter 13, skills and techniques will be provided for helping alienated parents express, explore, and experience their emotions in constructive ways.

...The rest of the chapter provides three different lists of typical emotions experienced by alienated parents ...

Typical Anxiety-Related Emotions Experienced by Alienated Parents

Affected	Doomed	Intense	Rubbery
Afraid	Edgy	Irritated	Scared
Alarmed	Embarrassed	Jittery	Self-conscious
Antsy	Fear	Jolted	Shaken
Anxious	Fearful	Knotted up	Shaky
Apprehension	Fidgety	Like jelly	Shocked
Apprehensive	Fixated	Melancholic	Shook-up
Awkward	Flustered	Melancholy	Sick
Bedeviled	Foolish	Mortified	Squeamish
Besieged	Frazzled	Nauseated	Squeezed
Blown	Fret-filled	Nerved up	Startled
Blown apart	Fretting	Nervous	Stiff
Blown away	Frightened	Nothing	Strained
Burdened	Gagged	Nuts	Stressed
Clammy	Ganged up on	Obsessed	Stressed out
Clenched	Hesitant	Obsessive	Tense
Closed in	Hindered	Off-center	Terrified
Concerned	Humiliated	Overanxious	Timid
Crazed	Ill	Overwhelmed	Traumatized
Crazy	Ill at ease	Overworked	Unassured
Dazed	Imbalanced	Panic	Uptight
Detached	Immense pressure	Panicky	Victimized
Disbelieving		Paralyzed	Volatile
Discomfort	Immobilized	Preoccupied	Vulnerable
Disoriented	Impatient	Pressured	Worried
Dissociated	Impeded	Quivery	Add Yours Here
Distressed	Inadequate	Re-traumatized	
Disturbed	In pain	Repulsed	
Dizzy	Insecure	Restless	

Typical Mood-Related Emotions Experienced by Alienated Parents

Aback	Blocked	Cursed	Desolate
Abandoned	Bludgeoned	Cut-off	Despair
Abashed	Blue	Damaged	Despaired
Abnormal	Boggled	Damned	Desperate
Absent-minded	Bored	Daunted	Despised
Afflicted	Bottled up	Dead	Despondent
Agonized	Broken	Debilitated	Detained
Agony	Broken-down	Deceived	Devastated
Alienated	Broken-hearted	Defeated	Devoid of
Alone	Broken-up	Defected	Digressing
Anguished	Bummed out	Defective	Diminished
Appalled	Burned out	Defenseless	Disappointed
Ashamed	Cast out	Deflated	Discarded
At a loss	Caught	Degraded	Discouraged
At fault	Censured	Dehumanized	Discredited
Awful	Cheerless	Dejected	Discriminated
Bad	Chewed up	Deleted	Discriminated Against
Badgered	Childless	Demolished	
Baffled	Choked up	Demonized	Disempowered
Battered	Chucked out	Demoralized	Disgraced
Belittled	Clouded	Denigrated	Disgruntled
Betrayed	Cloudy	Depleted	Disgusted
Bewildered	Clueless	Depreciated	Disheartened
Black-holed	Constrained	Depressed	Dished
Bland	Crappy	Deprived	Disillusioned
Bleak	Crucified	Derailed	Dismal
Bleeding	Cruddy	Desecrated	Dismayed
Blind	Crushed	Deserted	Dismissed

Typical Mood-Related Emotions Experienced by Alienated Parents *continued*			
Disowned	Electrified	Grave	Hung to dry
Disparaged	Embarrassed	Gray	Hung up
Displeased	Emotional	Grief	Hurried
Disposable	Emotionally bankrupt	Grief-stricken	Hurt
Disregarded		Grieving	Hyped up
Distraught	Emotionless	Grim	Hyper
Doomed	Empty	Grossed out	Hyper-vigilant
Doubted	Exasperated	Grouchy	Hyperactive
Doubtful	Excluded	Grumpy	Hysterical
Down	Excommunicated	Guilt	Icky
Down and out	Exhausted	Guilt-free	Idiotic
Down in dumps	Exiled	Guilt-tripped	Idle
Dragged down	Exploited	Guilty	Ignored
Drained	Fallen	Gullible	Imprisoned
Drawn back	Fatigued	Gutted	Inadequate
Dreaded	Fed up	Gypped	In a quandary
Dreadful	Flabbergasted	Haggard	Incapable
Dreary	Flawed	Halted	Incapacitated
Dried-up	Forgotten	Hard-pressed	Incoherent
Driven away	Forsaken	Heartbroken	Incommunicative
Driven out	Fractured	Hoaxed	Incompatible
Drowning	Fragile	Hollow	Incompetent
Dull	Fragmented	Hopeless	Incomplete
Dumbfounded	Frail	Horrified	Incongruent
Dying	Friendless	Horror-stricken	Inconsistent
Dysfunctional	Ghastly	Humiliated	Inconvenienced
Dysphoric	Gloomy	Humiliation	Incorrect
Dysthymic	Glum	Humility	Indecisive

Typical Mood-Related Emotions Experienced by Alienated Parents *continued*

Indefinite	Labeled	Mistrusted	Overruled
In despair	Lampooned	Misunderstood	Oversensitive
Indicted	Laughable	Mixed up	Paranoid
Indoctrinated	Left out	Moody	Passed by
In doubt	Lethargic	Moping	Passed over
Ineffective	Lied about	Muddled	Passed up
Ineffectual	Lied to	Nagged	Passionate
Inefficient	Lifeless	Nailed	Passive
Inept	Limited	Naive	Pathetic
Inequality	Listless	Needy	Pathologized
Inexperienced	Little	Negated	Peculiar
Inferior	Lonely	Negative	Perplexed
Inhibited	Lonesome	Neglected	Persecuted
Injured	Longing	Neurotic	Persuaded
In pity	Lost	Neutral	Perturbed
Insane	Lousy	Non-existent	Pessimistic
Inside-out	Low	Nonconforming	Pigeon-holed
Insignificant	Low spirited	Obliterated	Plagued
Insulted	Maladjusted	Offended	Pleading
Interfered with	Malaise	Out of it	Poisoned
Interrogated	Manic	Out of sorts	Pooped
Interrupted	Mind-shattered	Out of touch	Poorly
In the dumps	Miserable	Over-controlled	Possessed
In the way	Misguided	Over-zealous	Pouty
Intruded upon	Misinformed	Overcome	Pre-judged
Invalidated	Misrepresented	Overloaded	Preached to
Isolated	Mistaken	Overlooked	Precluded
Joyless	Mistreated	Overpowered	Prejudiced

Typical Mood-Related Emotions Experienced by Alienated Parents *continued*			
Pressed	Ridden	Sedentary	Sickened
Pressured	Ridiculed	Self-absorbed	Side-lined
Preyed upon	Ridiculous	Self-conscious	Silly
Probationed	Righteous	Self-critical	Singled-out
Propelled	Robotic	Self-deprecating	Sinking
Psychotic	Robot like		Skeptical
Pulled	Rotten	Self-pity	Sketchy
Pulled apart	Rough	Self-rejected	Skittish
Pursued	Ruffled	Self-righteous	Slain
Put down	Ruined	Self-sacrificing	Slandered
Puzzled	Run down	Self-serving	Sleepy
Questioned	Run over	Senile	Slighted
Questioning	Sacrificed	Sensitive	Slow
Ransacked	Sacrificial	Sentimental	Sluggish
Rattled	Sad	Separated	Smacked
Reflective	Sanctioned	Serious	Smacked down
Regressing	Sandpaper	Shamed	Small
Regretful	Satiated	Shameful	Sorrow
Rejected	Saturated	Shattered	Sorrowful
Remorse	Scapegoated	Sheepish	Sorry
Remorseful	Scarred	Shielded	Sour
Removed	Scattered	Shortchanged	Soured
Resentful	Scrutinized	Shouted out	Speechless
Resentment	Sealed in	Shredded	Spellbound
Resistant	Sealed off	Shut down	Spineless
Responsible	Second-guessing	Shut out	Spit on
Restricted		Shy	Spit out
Revolted	Second-rate	Sick at heart	Spooked

Typical Mood-Related Emotions Experienced by Alienated Parents *continued*			
Squashed	Subservient	Torn-apart	Useless
Stereotyped	Suffering	Tortured	Void
Stifled	Suicidal *	Trampled upon	Walls up
Stigmatized	Sulking	Turned off	Weak
Stirred	Sulky	Undesirable	Weary
Stirred up	Sullen	Unhappy	Wiped out
Strained	Sunk	Uninterested	Worn out
Stranded	Superseded	Unlovable	Worthless
Stretched	Susceptible	Unmotivated	Add Yours Here
Stricken	Suspicious	Unprepared	
Stubborn	Swamped	Unstable	
Stunned	Swindled	Unsupported	
Subordinate	Teary	Unwanted	
Subordinated	Tired	Used	

Important: If you have any thoughts of harming or killing yourself, please get medical assistance right away. Call your physician, call 911 (if available in your area) or go to your nearest hospital immediately.

Typical Anger-Related Emotions Experienced by Alienated Parents			
Abused	At war	Blackmailed	Combative
Accused	Ballistic	Blamed	Commanded
Aggravated	Battle-weary	Boiling	Condemned
Ambushed	Beaten	Bossed	Condescended
Angry	Beaten down	Brutalized	Connived
Anguish	Bedeviled	Bull-shitted	Conspired against
Annoyed	Befriended	Bullied	Controlled
Antagonized	Beseeched	Bushwhacked	Convicted
Argued with	Bitchy	Circumvented	Cornered
Assaulted	Bitter	Coaxed	Cranky
Attacked	Blacklisted	Coerced	Creeped out

Typical Anger-Related Emotions Experienced by Alienated Parents *continued*			
Criticized	Freaked out	Knocked down	Perturbed
Cross	Frenzied	Lambasted	Pestered
Cross-examined	Frustrated	Let down	Picked apart
Crossed	Fucked over	Ludicrous	Picked on
Crucified	Fucked up	Mad	Pissed
Defensive	Furious	Maddened	Pissed off
Defiant	Hammered	Maddening	Pissed on
Despised	Harassed	Manipulated	Pitted
Destroyed	Hardened	Mean	Played
Detested	Hated	Messed around	Provoked
Devoured	Hostile	Messed up	Pulverized
Dictated to	Hot-headed	Micro-managed	Pummeled
Disagreeable	Hot-tempered	Mind-fucked	Punched
Ditched	Hounded	Mistrustful	Punished
Dominated	Impatient	Nasty	Pushed
Domineered	In a stew	Neglected	Pushy
Double-crossed	Incensed	Nit-picked	Put down
Dumped	Incompetent	Nit-picky	Put out
Dumped on	Inflamed	Offensive	Quarrelsome
Duped	Infuriated	One-upped	Quashed
Enraged	Insulted	On the rebound	Radical
Envious	Intimidated	Opposed to	Raged
Evil	Irate	Oppositional	Raging
Explosive	Irked	Oppressed	Raided
Falsely accused	Irritable	Ornery	Railroaded
Fierce	Irritated	Ostracized	Raked
Fiery	Judged	Outdone	Raked over
Flip	Juiced up	Outlawed	Raped
Flip out	Justified	Outnumbered	Reactive
Fouled up	Kept at bay	Out powered	Reamed out
Framed	Kept away	Outraged	Rebellious
Fraught	Kept out	Paranoid	Reckless
Frazzled	Kicked around	Peeved	Repulsed

Typical Anger-Related Emotions Experienced by Alienated Parents *continued*			
Resentful	Seething	Squashed	Suckered
Retaliated against	Self-destructive	Squelched	Suspicious
Retaliation	Self-hate	Stalked	Thwarted
Revenge	Self-hatred	Stalled	Ticked off
Revengeful	Self-loathing	Steamed up	Upset
Ripped	Sentenced	Stepped on	Unstoppable
Ripped off	Set up	Stepped over	Vilified
Robbed	Shot down	Stern	Vindictive
Rough	Sinister	Stomped on	Whipped
Rowdy	Slaughtered	Stonewalled	Wounded
Ruthless	Snarky	Stopped	Add Yours Here
Sabotaged	Snarled at	Straight-jacketed	
Sadistic	Snowed	Strangled	
Sanctified	Snubbed	Strong-armed	
Scheming	Sold	Struck down	
Screwed	Sold out	Stuck	
Screwed over	Somber	Stunted	
Screwed up	Spent	Stupefied	
	Spiteful	Stymied	

Phew! That's a lot of feeling words listed in this chapter. It's surprising how many feeling words alienated parents have described to me throughout the years in clinical practice. Personally, I'm feeling a little overwhelmed right now from writing these lists! How about you? ✎

Time for Self-Reflection

What feelings are you experiencing from reading all the various types of emotions listed on the previous pages?

_____

_____

_____

_____

_____

_____

_____

_____

_____

_____

In what ways have you experienced an "emotional roller coaster ride" since PAS began?

_____

_____

_____

_____

_____

_____

_____

_____

_____

_____

_____

_____

_____

In what ways has your emotional roller coaster ride changed, if at all?

_____

_____

_____

_____

_____

_____

_____

_____

_____

_____

_____

Have you talked with other parents who have been alienated? If so, have they shared the types of feelings they've experienced? If so, what similarities and differences do you share with them?

_____

_____

_____

_____

_____

_____

_____

_____

_____

_____

_____

_____

_____

_____

_____

_____

_____

Additional notes:

_____

_____

_____

_____

_____

_____

_____

_____

_____

_____

_____

_____

_____

_____

_____

_____

Chapter Eleven
The Inevitability of Anger

*Anger is inevitable with mild,
moderate, or severe cases of PAS.
Quite frankly, I have never seen
any alienated child, alienated
parent, or alienating parent
escape the feelings of anger.
Let's consider this in greater depth.*

Anger is inevitable with mild, moderate, or severe cases of PAS. Quite frankly, I have never seen any alienated child, alienated parent, or alienating parent escape the feelings of anger. Let's consider this in greater depth.

All parents who fit the true definition for PAS share a common denominator: they all started off having a warm, loving relationship with their children prior to the start of the alienation. Once the alienation begins, they become the victims of an ongoing campaign of denigration, vilification, disloyalty, betrayal, opposition, mistreatment, and, in serious cases, absolute hatred and estrangement by their own children. The alienated parent is left in a captive position.

... All parents who fit the true definition for PAS share a common denominator: they all started off having a warm, loving relationship with their children prior to the start of the alienation ...

Alienating children tend to act as if their alienated parents have no emotions. I recall seeing a nine-year-old child who was vilifying her target mother say, "I like it so much when my mom cries. She deserves it and it makes me feel good." In this situation, like in so many others, the PAS target parent becomes a scapegoat; the indoctrinating parent has programmed the child to believe that if the target parent were to be utterly destroyed, then there will no longer be any problems within the family. Life will be sweet. Of course, that's not the case. Life is far from sweet for alienated parents as they experience an immense emotional roller coaster ride consisting of various negative emotions including varying degrees of anger.

In clinical practice, I've noticed an interesting commonality between alienated parents who reported being the spouse who initially brought up the subject of separation to their partner. In a large percentage of these cases, the partner used replies such as, "If you leave me, you'll never see our children again." Or, "If you don't want me or want to be married to me anymore, then you can't have our children either." Generally speaking, the alienating parent swears never having said such a statement. Nonetheless, their behaviors lend fortification to the target parent's assertion that such a threat was indeed made prior to the separation. The alienating parent reveals his or her own degree of anger by making such a strong claim against the target parent. It's at that moment in time that the campaign of denigration likely aids the alienating parent gain a sense of power, control, and revenge after feeling so hurt and rejected. From a rational perspective, however, this form of power, control, revenge, and anger is utterly pathological on the alienating parent's part. Not only is the alienating parent dismantling the bond between the other parent and their offspring, but the alienator programs and manipulates the children to inflict harm on the targeted parent, too.

... When the children's father or mother meets a new partner, it's not uncommon for the ex-partner to experience primary feelings of betrayal, disloyalty, and jealousy with the new partner ...

Jealousy seems to be another characteristic that tends to ignite PAS. When the children's father or mother meets a new partner, it's not uncommon for the ex-partner to experience primary feelings of betrayal, disloyalty, and jealousy with the new partner. Then secondary emotions kick in such as anger and possibly even rage. These types of feelings can easily ignite the start of PAS. One fellow, for example, stated, "That bitch left me for another man. I don't want my kids exposed to another man. She can't have them. I'll fight to have my kids all to myself." Another man I met years ago said, "She seems to have moved on with her life and is apparently getting married. That's not fair to my son living with some other guy instead of me. I'm his dad and that makes me irreplaceable. I'll show her she can't do that to me." A mother once said, "He's got a new girlfriend.

She's a pretty young thing. It must be nice that he has the time to run around and do that when I'm the one who primarily looks after the kids 24/7. So what if I try to get even and take him to the cleaners, he's the one who left me in the first place."

In the vast majority of cases, men continue to hold greater economic power over women today. During the separation, divorce, and/or post-divorce processes, many mothers living apart from their partners or ex-partners experience significant financial hardship, which in and of itself can ignite the start of PAS. These mothers may barely be able to afford to put food on the table so hiring an experienced, skilled attorney is out of the question. Driven by a sense of vulnerability and socio-economic inequality, it is not uncommon to see some mothers turn into alienators and program their children against their fathers.

...It is also not uncommon for alienating men to withhold spousal support and/or child support payments because they feel so enraged with anger ...

It is also not uncommon for alienating men to withhold spousal support and/or child support payments because they feel so enraged with anger. It's a way of getting even with the mother of the children. In these cases, PAS tends to escalate even further when the alienating father is court-mandated to make back payments for spousal and/or child support. Additionally, it is not uncommon when court-ordered to pay spousal and/or child support payments that the alienating father will suddenly fight for sole custody as a way to not have to pay the support. These types of battles tend to ensue for a very long time whereby the alienated children are the ones who really end up paying for it.

The Disneyland Dad phenomenon can also be quite present in PAS cases. There are three categorical types of Disneyland dads. The first type involves fathers who were never highly involved in their children's lives (for example those working long hours, or working out of town a lot) suddenly choose to want to become highly involved in their children's lives after the separation/divorce process. These kinds of dads turn themselves into alienating parents by their sudden over-involvement with the children, especially since most of the target mothers have no choice but to work full-time hours creating less time to be with their children.

The second type also involves fathers who were never highly involved in their children's lives prior to the separation/divorce process but do so afterwards plus they also have the economic means to lure their children through bribery to become alienated. In these kinds of PAS cases, the children have become baited and turn against the other parent. These types of Disneyland dads buy their alienated children expensive gifts, take them on expensive trips, and so forth.

The third type involves fathers who were significantly involved in their children's lives prior to the separation/divorce process. They become Disneyland dads when their children's primary residence is with their mother. As a way to "settle the score" in an attempt to overcompensate for not spending as much time with their children, these fathers tend to lure and bait their children into alienation through bribery. This form of the Disneyland Dad phenomenon is very apparent when the children's mother cannot afford what he can. Thus, the children are not only lured by the alienating father's economic power but may also be told that, "Mommy will never be able to buy you a car when you turn sixteen like I can." Or "Mommy will never be able to afford to own a house with a built-in swimming pool like I have." Or "Those clothes you're wearing look like something a street person would wear. Here's $250.00. Let's go shopping and buy you some nice stuff."

In more recent time, the term Hostile Aggressive Parenting (HAP) (Family Conflict Resolution Services, 2006) has been used in conjunction with PAS. It is important to keep in mind that HAP and PAS are not equivalent in terms of meanings, however. Accordingly,

> *... The second type also involves fathers who were never highly involved in their children's lives prior to the separation/divorce process ...*

"HAP refers to the behaviors, actions and decisions of a person, whereas, PAS relates to the psychological condition of the child. In the vast majority of cases HAP is the cause of PAS" (Family Conflict Resolution Services, 2006, p. 5). Similar to PAS, HAP is a form of child abuse that tends to occur in high-conflict separation and toxic divorce battles. Nonetheless, parents who show evidence of HAP tend to use a broad array "of hostile and aggressive tactics designed to make life difficult for the friendly parent and to disrupt their child's relationship with the friendlier parent" (p. 33). Parents who fall under the category of HAP tend to engage in anti-social, bullying behaviors that can, at times, be considered extremely intense and violent. Some examples of the severe type of HAP include, but are not limited to, falsifying court documents, concocting anonymous allegations of abuse involving the other parent and their child to the police and child protection agencies, exposing their children to sexual activities with a new partner, engaging in various acts of property crime such as destroying the other parent's vehicle or home, coercing their children to use prescription drugs to alter the child's personality or behaviors, threatening or intimidating third parties who are trying to help the children, and continuing to exhibit tremendous anger and rage toward the other parent for years after separating (Family Conflict Resolution Services, 2006).

...Parents who fall under the category of HAP tend to engage in anti-social, bullying behaviors that can, at times, be considered extremely intense and violent ...

It's Not What You Have. It's What You Do With What You Have!

Let's explore some important aspects about anger. First and foremost, anger can serve a useful, adaptive, constructive purpose or it can serve a useless, non-adaptive, deconstructive purpose throughout our lives. In other words, "It is not what you have, but it's what you do with what you have."

There are many positive functions of anger. For example, anger can help facilitate your expression of tension, conflict, and negative feelings. Anger is a signal that a problem exists which is causing you discomfort, distress, grief, pain, suffering, or even anguish. It may be environmental, interpersonal, or intrapersonal. Anger can act as a signal that tells you that it's time to deal with the distress. Anger can give you instant energy and prepare your own body for self-defense. Anger provides you with stamina. Another positive function of anger is it can help you feel more empowered and help you be in charge of yourself.

On the downside, there are many negative functions of anger. Here are a few examples. Anger can disrupt and warp your thoughts and actions through arousal. Anger can be used to avoid other feelings by defending yourself when it's not called for or needed. Anger can quickly lead to aggression, especially the aggressive-exploding type of anger. You probably know what I mean by the latter type of anger. Have you ever met someone who is the aggressive-exploding type? This is the individual who acts like a pressure cooker or a volcano. During the initial phase, the person tries to hold his or her anger in because there's a danger of letting off steam all at once. But, sooner or later the pressure mounts, it becomes impossible to hold in any longer, and their anger is explosive and very destructive.

... Anger can disrupt and warp your thoughts and actions through arousal ...

There are three types of passive styles of anger that have very negative functions. First, the somatizing type of anger is like having acid in your body. The term somatize refers to expressing psychological conflicts through various physical or body symptoms. And, unfortunately but true, the somatizing type of anger is linked to the development of at least twenty different medical conditions ranging from headaches to certain types of cancer. With this type of anger, resentment is the key feeling you likely admit to having. And, you will tend to ruminate on past hurts and imagined threats.

Then there's the self-punishing type of passive anger. If you fall into this category, then you are really good at beating up your own self-concept. You blame yourself and demand more of yourself. In other words, you are your own worst enemy!

The third passive type of anger is called underhanding. It's the least obvious type but nevertheless very destructive and harmful. It involves using sarcasm, gossip, teasing, sharing secrets, pouting, or obstructive acts such as forgetting to give someone a message or sabotaging group efforts.

There are numerous other purposes of anger that may seem like you are winning but it tends to create a lose-lose situation instead. Does anger make you feel powerful and help you stay in control of situations and others? If so, it's a way to mask your own fears and insecurities. Does your anger help produce enough energy to get things done? If so, then it likely ends up producing opposition from others and you will likely feel physically wiped out after a while. Perhaps you use anger to avoid communication, sharing, and intimacy, especially in fearful areas of life. Do you use anger as protection to feel safe or to establish boundaries? Or, do you use anger as a way of asserting you're right? Many individuals would rather be right than happy. Maybe your use of anger is to make others feel guilty. Or, your anger helps you avoid feelings that are underneath it such as fear, frustration, or hurt. Anger can also be used to hold on to a relationship and to avoid feeling loneliness, especially through resentment of your partner or another family member. Do you use anger to stay in the role of victim? If so, then you expect the world to change instead of taking responsibility for yourself. Or, do you use anger to avoid taking responsibility for what is actually occurring in your life right now?

With anger, you choose the response depending upon your own parental modeling and what you believe will pay off. Please keep in mind that anger is usually an expression of unmet expectations and unexamined personal beliefs, values, and morals. ❧

...Do you use anger as protection to feel safe or to establish boundaries? Or, do you use anger as a way of asserting you're right? ...

Time for Self-Reflection

List some positive functions your own anger has served:

_____
_____
_____
_____
_____
_____
_____
_____

List some negative functions your own anger has served:

_____
_____
_____
_____
_____
_____
_____
_____

Can you think of any other purposes your anger has served?

_____
_____
_____
_____
_____
_____
_____
_____

What is the nature of your anger? How are you experiencing anger emotionally? Are you generally an aggressive-exploding type, a somatizing type, or a combination?

_____

_____

_____

_____

_____

_____

_____

_____

What words are most appropriate that describe your anger? For example, do you feel irked, frustrated, bitter, betrayed, resentful, mad, pissed off, furious, enraged, or something else? Check the list of anger-related emotions in chapter 10, pages 128 to 130 if you like.

_____

_____

_____

_____

_____

_____

_____

Do you tend to notice where your anger manifests itself in your body? For example, do you feel your heart racing, sweating, muscle tension, fatigue? If you haven't noticed it before, try to notice it next time you feel angry and list it here.

_____

_____

_____

_____

_____

How did your parents use their anger? How did they role-model it to you?

_____

_____

_____

_____

_____

_____

_____

_____

Do you use anger in the same way it was role-modeled by your parents? What similarities and/or differences do you notice?

_____

_____

_____

_____

_____

_____

_____

_____

What do you notice about your alienated child's anger?

_____

_____

_____

_____

_____

_____

_____

_____

Has the nature and degree of your child's anger changed since being alienated? If so, describe in what ways. Please be specific.

_____

_____

_____

_____

_____

_____

_____

_____

_____

What have you noticed about your ex-partner's anger?

_____

_____

_____

_____

_____

_____

Has the nature and degree of your ex-partner's anger seemed to have changed since the beginning of the alienation process? If so, describe in what ways. Please be specific.

_____

_____

_____

_____

_____

_____

_____

The Twelve Most Common Mistakes
Alienated Parents Tend To Make With Their Children

There are at least twelve common mistakes that alienated parents tend to make when feeling angry and in contact via phone, letter writing, social networking, or in person with their alienated children. Here are some suggestions to help offset this from occurring in your family. They are:

1. When in contact with your children don't trash, bash, berate, put down, or persecute their other parent. Doing so, you are modeling abusive behavior to your children. This will ultimately backfire on you. Your children will likely feel very uncomfortable and have less respect for you. Additionally, this kind of behavior on your part will likely push them further away from you.

2. Don't challenge or dispute your children's loyalty to the alienating parent. Choosing to do so will only create more resistance. Remember, the greater you challenge your children's loyalty to the other parent, the more your children will resist. Be encouraging and focus on the positive aspects of their relationship. For example, stated in a warm and sincere manner, "I'm impressed with the way you take such good care of your father."

... Don't challenge or dispute your children's loyalty to the alienating parent. Choosing to do so will only create more resistance ...

3. Don't discuss any legal information. It's important that your children do not hear any references to court actions or any other legal information. This includes not showing them any legal or court documents. Don't be surprised if your older children or teens insist that you share legal information with them to help sort out what is true and what is not. Keep in mind that legal information including the difficult language, what court orders actually mean, and so on can be difficult for most adults to comprehend, never mind children and teens.

Confusing court documents may encourage children to take sides; redirect them instead.

4. In spite of sounding counter-intuitive, don't make demands. For example, "What you should do is treat me with respect instead of treating me with such disrespect. I'm your parent so don't talk to me that way." Even though your likely intention is to attempt to control the situation with your alienated child and provide some prompt remedy, what it really says to your alienated child is this: "You don't have the right to decide how to deal with your issues and feelings." Remember, your child is a victim, as well. Your child has not intentionally created PAS; your child has been drawn into it by his/her other parent.

...It is perfectly okay to clarify any misconceptions that your alienated children may have about you or your situation ...

5. Don't interrogate. For example, "What did your mom say to you to make you say that to me?" Although you may have good intentions to get to the bottom of the issue and find out what was said or done to make your child react the way he/she has to you, it will backfire. What it really says to your alienated child is, "Not only your mother but you must have messed up here." This will only make your children feel worse and they will likely reject you more. Please note: It is perfectly okay to clarify any misconceptions that your alienated children may have about you or your situation. For example, if your child says, "Daddy says you never loved him or us," you can say, for instance, "Sorry sweetie, the moment we met, I fell in love with your father. You and your brother were loved from the moment we knew you were going to be born. I will never stop loving you no matter what." Whenever the need arises to clarify any misconceptions that your alienated children may have about you or your situation, remind them of specific memories you have about them or of other people, places, times, or things

related to their misconceptions. This would be a great time to share any photographs or videos you may have of those times.

6. Don't moralize. For example, "The right thing to say to me is .....", "You really should ....", "It's wrong to ....". Although the likely intention is to show your child the proper way to deal with the issue, the meaning of the message is, "I'll choose your values for you." This will backfire too.

7. Don't pretend to act like a psychologist. For example, "Do you know why you said that to me? You're just copying your mother. That's what she always says, you know." Even though your likely intention is to help prevent future issues by analyzing your child's behavior and explaining his/her motives, what it really says to your child is, "I know more about you than you know about yourself. And, that makes me superior to you." It'll backfire because your alienated child will not feel like a social equal which will likely push him/her even further away from you.

8. Don't yell, scream, nag, coax, lecture, or give ultimatums. All children don't like to be yelled or screamed at. Nor do they like to be nagged, coaxed, lectured, or given ultimatums by their parents. They feel disrespected and tend to counter it by disrespecting the parent back. The same holds true for alienated children but generally to a greater degree. For example, "How dare you speak to me in that tone of voice. If you do that again, then I don't want you to come around here anymore." This kind of behavior on your part will likely induce fear in your alienated child. The child may interpret these types of messages as truth, whether you mean it or not. Your children may actually use this as a way to avoid seeing you again. It'll make it much more difficult for you and your

> *... Don't yell, scream, nag, coax, lecture, or give ultimatums. All children don't like to be yelled or screamed at. Nor do they like to be nagged, coaxed, lectured, or given ultimatums by their parents...*

alienated child to repair the relationship.

9. Don't use guilt trips. For example, "You wouldn't really treat me the way you do now if I earned as much money as your father does." Although your likely intention is to help your child see the wrong in his/her thoughts, feelings, and actions, what it really says to your child is, "I am imposing a penance for your past mistakes because you and your other parent are at fault." Imposing guilt on the rampage also backfires.

10. Don't deny your children's feelings and only justify yours. For example, "Oh, that's not true. You don't really feel upset. If anybody should feel upset, it should be me." Alienated children need to have their feelings validated just as much as anybody else does. Although it's quite unlikely that your children will validate your feelings due to the level of PAS that is occurring, please don't let that stop you from role-modeling it to them. It will be of help in repairing your broken relationship.

..Don't be stubborn and child-like. Apologize for mistakes you have made now and in the past. As you're aware, alienated parents undergo a vast array of negative emotions including anger ...

11. Don't be stubborn and child-like. Apologize for mistakes you have made now and in the past. As you're aware, alienated parents undergo a vast array of negative emotions including anger. Although it may be very difficult to do, it's not impossible to apologize to your alienated children when you have intentionally, unintentionally, or unknowingly done something wrong now or in the past. We want to teach our children to be responsible, caring, and accountable people when they grow up. What is stopping us from role-modeling that to them? It's okay to say, for instance, "I realize that there were many times when I had to work evenings and weekends and I wasn't able to go to your school concerts and soccer games. I apologize for not being there."

12. Don't react or over-react when your children treat you

with criticism, contempt, defensiveness, or stonewalling. It's very important to learn to be proactive and active rather than reactive and over-reactive with them. As difficult as it will be, it is so very important for you to do your very best and develop a hard shell like a tortoise! If you were to react or over-react, then your alienated children will likely feel no need to ever want to repair the fragmented relationship. ☙

Sometimes an alienated parent will unleash anger on his or her children and forget that they are victims, too.

...Don't react or over-react when your children treat you with criticism, contempt, defensiveness, or stonewalling ...

Time for Self-Reflection

Here's a friendly reminder: All parents make mistakes. When filling out this section of the workbook, please be gentle on yourself. Remember: Mistakes are for learning!

List some mistakes that you have made in the past with your alienated child or children:

_____

_____

_____

_____

_____

_____

_____

_____

_____

_____

_____

How have you tried to rectify those mistakes, if at all?

_____

_____

_____

_____

_____

_____

_____

_____

_____

_____

_____

_____

List some ideas you have to help overcome any of the twelve most common mistakes that alienated parents tend to make with their children:

_____

_____

_____

_____

_____

_____

_____

_____

_____

_____

_____

_____

_____

_____

_____

_____

The following three chapters will offer additional strategies on how to deal more effectively with angry thoughts, feelings, and actions.

Chapter Twelve
Get Rid of Counter-
productive Thinking

Now that we have explored the numerous types of feelings that alienated parents generally experience, it's time to explore the types of negative thinking that occur alongside various negative feelings.

Now that we have explored the numerous types of feelings that alienated parents generally experience, it's time to explore the types of negative thinking that occur alongside various negative feelings. Notice that the term being used here is called counterproductive thinking, which ultimately creates a lose-lose situation.

First and foremost, let's take a look at the Think, Feel, Do, and Consequences Sequence. When you get caught up in any emotion, it appears as if someone or something is making you feel that way. The person or event is, in other words, deliberately causing you emotional pain. However, none of this is true. You see, what really occurs is a triggering effect. Something unpleasant happens; your buttons are pushed by external triggers such as your ex-spouse phones when least expected and provides news you're not prepared to hear; or, your buttons are pushed by internal triggers such as fatigue, lack of energy, hunger, dehydration, sickness, and so forth.

...When you get caught up in any emotion, it appears as if someone or something is making you feel that way ...

Next, come thoughts. You evaluate and think to yourself, "What a jerk! This is crap! How awful! It's unfair! I don't deserve this! He'll pay for this!"

Then your feelings arise. You may feel hurt, rejected, betrayed, attacked, ridiculed, mad, scared, and so forth.

Your behavior comes next in sequence. You act out your feelings by running, fighting, attacking, crying, seeking revenge, withdrawing, avoiding, etc.

And lastly, there are consequences. Negative thoughts, feelings, and behaviors will produce negative consequences whereas positive thoughts, feelings, and behaviors will produce positive consequences. It's impossible for negative thoughts, feelings, and behaviors to produce positive consequences just as it's impossible for positive thoughts, feelings, and behaviors to produce negative consequences.

The Think, Feel, Do, Consequences Sequence

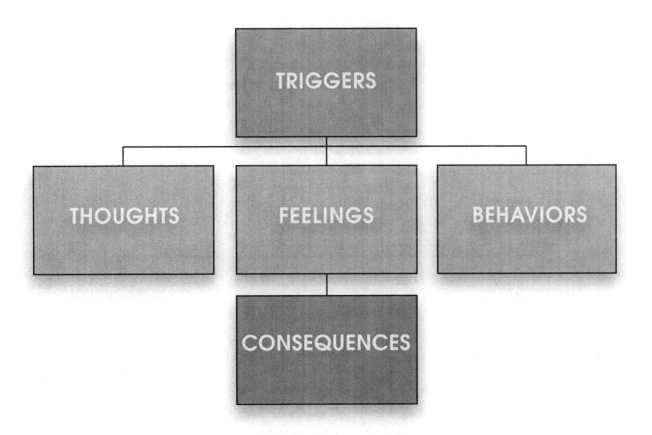

Jamie's Example:

Myra's Example:

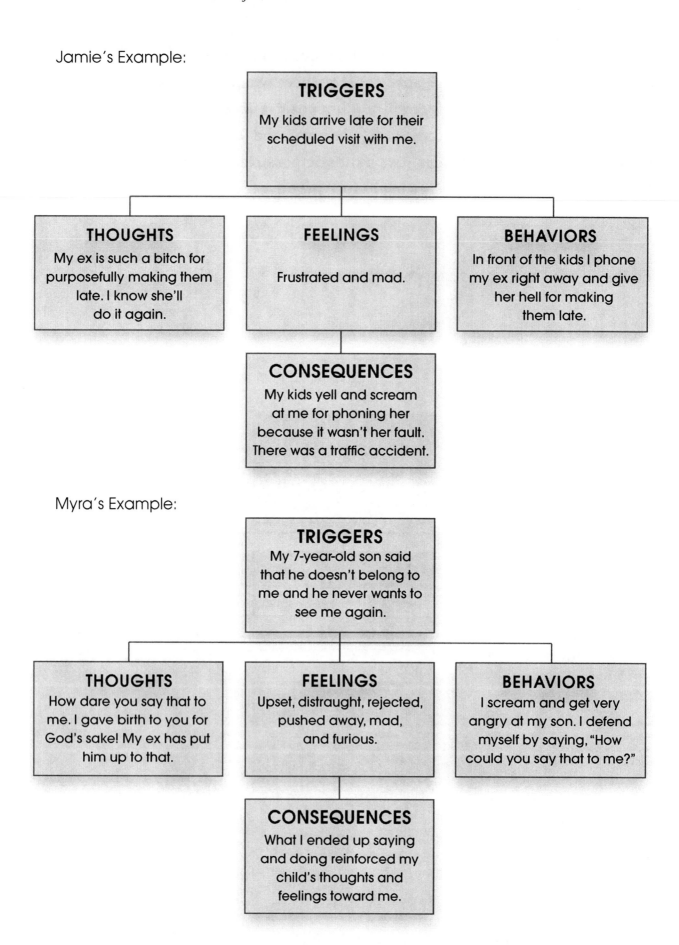

Time for Self-Reflection

Think of a recent time you were triggered by a situation or event pertaining to PAS. Write down what triggered you, what you were thinking, what you were feeling, what you did, and what the consequences of your actions were.

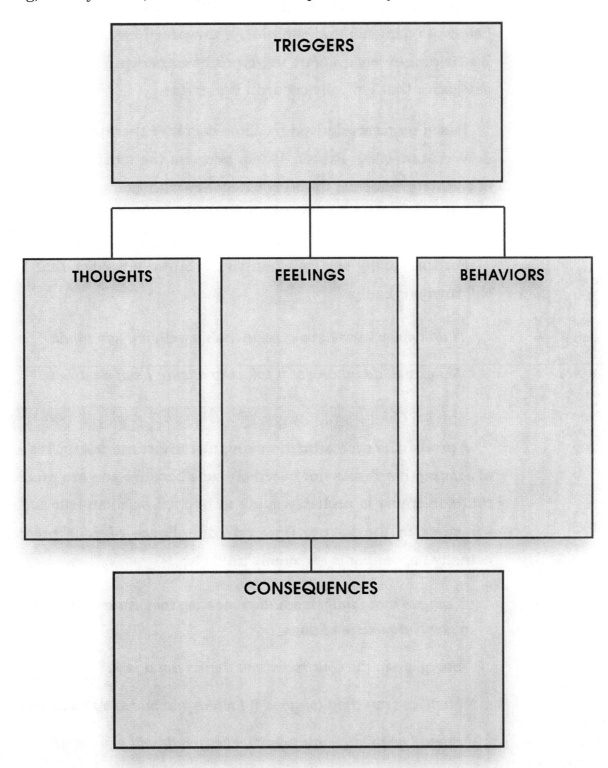

Counterproductive Thinking and PAS

As you can probably see, your thoughts play such a fundamental role in generating certain feelings and escalating them. The combination of your thoughts and feelings cause you to choose (unconsciously, unknowingly, or consciously) to engage in certain behaviors (actions) and ultimately, unwanted consequences occur. It's helpful to learn about the types of counterproductive thinking categories that typically occur in PAS cases.

Based on terms derived by some cognitive therapy experts (Beck & Weishaar, 1989; Burns, 1999), here are the most common types of counterproductive thinking categories with examples:

Fortune-Telling

Fortune-telling occurs when you arbitrarily predict that things will turn out badly:

"I will never ever have a relationship with my son again."

"My ex will do whatever it takes to ensure I self-destruct."

Probability Overestimations

A probability overestimation is similar to fortune-telling. It's a type of assumption that is not based on facts because you are predicting that something is probably going to happen or come true today or sometime in the future. However, the chance of your prediction actually happening is extremely unlikely:

"Going to that family mediation meeting tomorrow is going to be a complete waste of time."

"Everyone in the courtroom will think I am a jerk."

"I will lose my child for good if I make just one simple mistake."

"When I go to my son's school, everybody will glare at me."

... The combination of your thoughts and feelings cause you to choose (unconsciously, unknowingly, or consciously) to engage in certain behaviors (actions) and ultimately, unwanted consequences occur ...

Overgeneralizations

An overgeneralization occurs when you view a negative event as a never-ending pattern of defeat:

"This court battle over custody will never end."

"Things like this always happen to me."

"I cannot survive life without my children."

Mind-reading

Mind-reading occurs when you arbitrarily assume that people are reacting negatively to you:

"The judge will think I'm a freak if he sees my hands shaking."

"My relatives must think I am crazy because my kids don't want to see me anymore."

"Everyone always knows when I am feeling in despair."

... Mind-reading occurs when you arbitrarily assume that people are reacting negatively to you ...

Misattributions/Single Explanations

Misattributions/single explanations are similar to mind-reading. When you feel any type of negative emotion such as hurt, fear, anxiety, or anger, it's easy to suppose that it was deliberately done on purpose and, of course, meant to upset you. Then you likely start jumping to conclusions and making assumptions about the other person's actual motives:

"I'm sure my ex is still pissed off with me for having an affair during our marriage and that's why she is doing this to get to me."

"My kid embarrassed me at the soccer park just to make me look stupid."

"He did that to make me angry."

Mental Filter

A mental filter occurs when you dwell on the negatives and ignore the positives:

"I'm a bad father."

"It's all my fault because I never spent enough time with my kids."

"How could I have been such an awful mother all those years?"

Discounting the Positives

Discounting the positives occurs when you insist that your accomplishments or positive qualities don't count:

"Thanks for the compliments but if you only knew what I'm really like, then you wouldn't say those nice things about my parenting."

"I'm the worst parent in the world and deserve what's happened."

"I tried to visit my kids last night, but one night out of 30 doesn't count for much."

... Discounting the positives occurs when you insist that your accomplishments or positive qualities don't count ...

Emotional Reasoning

Emotional reasoning occurs when you reason from how you feel:

"I feel guilty so I must be guilty."

"I feel like such an idiot, so I guess I am."

"I'm such a loser."

All or Nothing Thinking

All or nothing thinking occurs when you look at things in absolute, black and white categories rather than recognizing that some things or situations can't be pigeonholed:

"I'm a bad parent."

"If I say just one thing wrong, I will blow my entire chance of ever seeing Jimmy again."

"If I don't look like I have it all together during the court trial, then my attorney is going to think I'm stupid."

"Revealing any signs of anxiety in front of the judge is just as awful as falling apart completely."

Inflammatory/Global Labeling

Global labeling occurs when you make negative judgments about yourself or others. Some common global labels include words like: idiot, stupid, selfish, loser, jerk, fuck-up, and so on. Rather than focus on a specific behavior, you incriminate the entire individual. Global labels are never true given they amplify a single characteristic and imply that it's the whole picture:

"Your father is a complete screw-up and failure."

"That bastard can go to hell."

"I made mistakes in parenting and I'm a loser."

"Dad, why are you always so selfish?"

"All attorneys are uncaring jerks!"

... Global labeling occurs when you make negative judgments about yourself or others ...

Should Statements

Should statements occur when you criticize yourself or other people using words like: should, shouldn't, must, must not, ought to, ought not, have to:

"She should pay for this mess we're all in!"

"I should never make any parenting mistakes again."

"My friends should never think badly about my losses."

"From now on I have to do everything perfectly because I may never have another shot at this again."

"A competent attorney should be able to get rid of my pain and agony."

Personalization

Personalization occurs when you blame yourself for something you were not entirely responsible for:

"My kids wouldn't be alienated if I hadn't screwed up so badly in earlier years."

"The fact that my ex and kids left me is proof that I'm incompetent."

"While standing in the elevator at the courthouse, this woman was looking at me and likely thinking that I'm strange."

"I am being punished by God for something I did wrong."

Blaming

Blame occurs when you blame other people and overlook ways that you contributed to the problem:

"My ex is entirely responsible for causing this high-conflict court battle."

"My ex and kids have caused all my anguish and have no idea how hurt and rejected they make me feel."

"I could enjoy life if it weren't for this alienation problem."

Commanding/Demanding

Commanding or demanding occurs when you raise the level of expectations for yourself, others, and the world in general:

"Just wait until I talk to my son next. I'll tell him that he needs to love, approve, and respect me just like he does his mother."

"How can you say that to me? I'm your mother and you need to show me some respect right now!"

... Blame occurs when you blame other people and overlook ways that you contributed to the problem ...

"I shouldn't have to deal with all this pain, frustration, and delay by the attorneys."

"It's just not right that my ex turned my kid against me."

"My ex's attorney shouldn't express any disapproval or criticism against me."

"It's not right that it has to take so long for the courts to get on with my case. I am entitled to custody."

Magnifying/Catastrophizing

Magnifying or catastrophizing occurs when you assume that if a negative event or situation was to actually occur, it would be absolutely awful, terrible, and insurmountable. You have probably heard the expression, "making a mountain out of a molehill." In other words, you may be thinking that a situation is much worse than it really is:

"It would be awful to lose my train of thought during a family mediation meeting."

"My life is a complete disaster."

"This is a totally screwed up life!"

"My pain is totally unbearable."

> *... Minimization occurs when you shrink the importance of what is actually happening or will happen in the future ...*

Minimization

Minimization occurs when you shrink the importance of what is actually happening or will happen in the future. Denial is also a form of minimization:

"There's no need to force my alienated child into having any contact with me. I'll let it go. Life is too short."

"He'll grow up someday and see the light."

"There's no need to seek professional help with a counselor. I can do this on my own. It's not that big a deal."

"All teenagers hate their parents, so what's the big deal?"

Perfectionism

Perfectionism occurs when you think that you, others, and the world should be perfect, flawless, and right. Individuals who hold these kinds of unrealistic standards for themselves, others, or the world tend to have overly rigid thinking and tend to experience a lot of unhappiness and stress:

> *"My family was perfect until my marriage fell apart and this PAS thing happened."*

> *"My life will be a breeze once we no longer experience any family alienation."*

> *"I cannot afford to make any mistakes."*

... Perfectionism occurs when you think that you, others, and the world should be perfect, flawless, and right ...

Selective Attention

Selective attention occurs when you generally pay more attention to certain types of information over other types:

> *"My ex has asked me to return our son home a day early on my weekend with him."* (Even though she has offered an extra day at another time).

It's well established that we don't pay attention to everything around us. Here's an illustration. Outside a courtroom during a morning break, there may be a lot of people talking around you while you are having a one-on-one conversation with your attorney. And, although it may seem that you've filtered everything else out, someone mentions your name in another conversation across the hall; you immediately tune in to that conversation.

Selective Memory

Selective memory occurs when you generally remember certain types of information more so than others:

"The judge looked really bored when it was my attorney's turn to defend me." (However, you ignored the judge when he appeared to be enlightened by some things your attorney said.)

"I recall being teased in elementary school and being alienated feels very similar." (Even though you forget about all the good times you spent with friends in elementary school as well as with your own children.)

Perhaps you're now asking yourself, "How do I stop this vicious negative think-feel-do-consequences cycle as well as my counterproductive thinking?" Chapter 13 offers numerous strategies to help you with this. ❧

... How do I stop this vicious negative think-feel-do-consequences cycle as well as my counter-productive thinking? ...

Time for Self-Reflection:

List the types of counterproductive thinking categories that you typically use on a regular basis. Provide an example of how you've used each one.

Category:_____

Examples:_____

_____

_____

Category:_____

Examples:_____

_____

_____

Category:_____

Examples:_____

_____

_____

Do you feel surprised or not about the number of counterproductive thinking categories that you generally use? Please explain.

What are the possible costs of choosing to continue to engage in this vicious negative think-feel-do-consequences cycle as well as your counterproductive thinking?

For the majority of alienated parents, the benefits of overcoming this vicious negative cycle and counterproductive thinking using strategies that are offered in this book far outweigh the costs. Take a look at the following examples of possible benefits and place a checkmark in the box if you think this may benefit you:

❑ I may improve the quality of my relationships.

❑ I may meet new friends.

❑ I may learn to increase my enjoyment of life.

❑ I may increase my ability to express myself.

❑ I may learn to feel more comfortable in feared social situations.

❑ I may learn to feel more comfortable in performance situations.

❑ I may learn to confront certain people or situations better.

❑ I may feel more comfortable in situations related to my job or career.

❑ I may learn new strategies that I may be able to apply to other problems, including anger, depression, anxiety, or other troubles.

❑ I may feel more self-confident.

❑ I may be able to improve my job or educational prospects.

❑ I may be able to expand on other opportunities for areas of self-improvement.

❑ I may be able to expand other possible options for what I can do in my leisure time.

Now that you have had an opportunity to consider the benefits of working on overcoming your counterproductive thinking patterns, you are in a better position to make a commitment to working on overcoming them. If you feel committed to moving forward, it would be a good idea to set some general and specific goals or objectives. Specific goals are more detailed than general goals and are easier for you to measure progress and take pride in your accomplishments. I encourage you to generate as many specific goals as possible. Please ensure they are realistic. It's also important to determine whether you want to accomplish short-term (what you'd like to accomplish this week), medium-term (what you want to accomplish over the next few months), or long-term (what you want to accomplish over the next year or two) goals.

Here's an example:

General Goal	Specific Goal
To increase my friendships.	I will meet at least two new friends within six months, with whom I can watch sports, TV, eat out, and go to movies.
To cope better with my ex and child's negative remarks to me.	To be able to tolerate negative feedback each time I have contact with my ex and child without becoming very upset and angry toward them.

It's your turn to think about what kinds of realistic changes you would like to make.

My realistic general and specific short-term goals are:

_____

_____

_____

_____

_____

_____

_____

My realistic general and specific medium-term goals are:

_____

_____

_____

_____

_____

My realistic general and specific long-term goals are:

_____

_____

_____

_____

_____

_____

Do you see any possible benefits at all? When answering these questions, consider how overcoming or not overcoming your counterproductive thinking patterns may have an impact on all the following areas of your life: work, friendships, family relationships, self-confidence, self-expression, learning to feel more comfortable in feared situations, and leisure time.

_____

_____

_____

_____

_____

_____

_____

_____

_____

_____

_____

_____

_____

_____

_____

_____

_____

Chapter Thirteen
It's the Productive Thought that Counts

Each and every one of us owns a unique pair of opaque subjective glasses that are based on our own genetic predispositions and environmental experiences from growing up. Our own unique subjective glasses are not necessarily accurate!

By now you likely realize that your thoughts are not always what they seem. In other words, they are mainly assumptions that are not based on facts for the most part! Yet each and every day, we humans assume that the thoughts going through our heads are mostly true, and that we have all the information we need to inform our thinking and make choices. Wow! That's profound, isn't it!

On a more serious note, it's very important to take into account that, among all the things that you have learned since early childhood, you might have acquired certain thoughts or beliefs that are neither true nor precise. As a matter of fact, some of your thoughts and beliefs may be utterly damaging and cause you to see yourself, others, life, and the world in a counterproductive and distorted manner. The latter statement does not mean that there is something wrong with you or that you're not smart. It just means that sometimes you may get overly attached to your thoughts and beliefs that you were exposed to in your early childhood and are not aware that there are other ways to think, believe, and view the world. Each and every one of us owns a unique pair of opaque subjective glasses that are based on our own genetic predispositions and environmental experiences from growing up. Our own unique subjective glasses are not necessarily accurate!

Each and every member of an alienated family will engage in the various types of counterproductive thinking errors (as discussed in chapter 12) with respect to the alienation and other issues. Can you see how these errors create problems within the dynamics of the alienated family? The following suggestions will help you learn how to overcome counterproductive thinking and learn how to think more productively or rationally, which will help you have more positive feelings. Then you will likely want to engage in more positive behaviors with positive consequences.

How to Talk Yourself out of Counterproductive Thinking, Feel Better and Enhance Your Overall Well-Being

Important: It is highly recommended that you learn and apply these skills in a linear step-by-step fashion.

Tip #1

Find a quiet space where you will not be disturbed. Study and memorize the "Think, Feel, Do, Consequences Sequence" discussed in chapter 12 to help become totally familiar and mindful of it. In doing so, you will have a much better chance at overcoming counterproductive thinking.

... The following suggestions will help you learn how to overcome counter-productive thinking and learn how to think more productively or rationally, which will help you have more positive feelings ...

Tip #2

Once you have read and understand the material from Tip #1, name and briefly describe the most common types of counterproductive thinking patterns you tend to engage in. Refer to chapter 12 for a review of the most common types that alienated parents tend to use. For example, if you observe yourself using a lot of magnifying, then write magnifying down below and give an example of it. For instance, *"Yesterday, I thought it was the end of the world because my daughter told me to shut up over the phone."* Write them here:

_____

_____

_____

_____

_____

_____

_____

_____

_____

_____

_____

... Each and every day, practice identifying the types of counter-productive thinking errors you may be using ...

Tip #3

Each and every day, practice identifying the types of counterproductive thinking errors you may be using. Obviously, you will need to memorize them! It shouldn't be too hard memorizing them all! Keep practicing catching yourself using one or more types of counterproductive thinking errors. You may also catch other people doing the same thing! Remember, mistakes are for learning so please be gentle on yourself. Do this step often for the first couple of weeks and, as you become familiar, you will eventually end up being less and less counterproductive in your thinking. Trust me! It will happen if you persist with this step.

Tip #4

As often as possible, use a third eye so to speak, and practice catching yourself using one or more types of counterproductive thinking such as overgeneralizations, personalization, mind-reading, selective attention, and so on. Notice the key words or phrases that you generally use. For example, do you use a lot of 'should' statements? Also, if you notice yourself using the same words or phrases repeatedly, it's best to jot them down on a notepad, a journal, or record them in the notes section of your cell phone. This will serve as a friendly reminder and start helping you set off some alarm bells along the way! It is highly recommended that you write things down so that you can accurately reflect on and shift your counterproductive thinking.

Tip #5

After practicing what you have learned in tips 1 through 4, do a check-in with yourself and ask the following question: Do I feel reasonably comfortable in observing and identifying the common types of counterproductive thinking errors I'm using? If you answered yes, then it sounds like you're ready to move on. But, if you answered no, please don't feel badly about yourself. All you need to do is reread the descriptions of the counterproductive thinking patterns and keep plugging along at observing, identifying, and writing them down. Discovering these types of thinking errors have to become second nature to you. For some people, it takes a little longer to become an expert at noticing them. There's no expected time line to learn this, no exams, and no grades being given to achieve this. Keep practicing and, before you know it, you'll get it!

... There's no expected time line to learn this, no exams, and no grades being given to achieve this. Keep practicing and, before you know it, you'll get it...

Tip #6

It's time for you to go back to your list of the types of counterproductive thinking errors you tend to engage in. It's a good idea to review it to refresh your memory. Next, for each one of your counterproductive thinking errors, try to come up with alternative thoughts or interpretations to your original one. If you're thinking, "Easier said than done!" you're right. But remember, you have accomplished a lot so far by memorizing and identifying the types you use. So give yourself a big hug or pat on the back and tell yourself you can do it!

... give yourself a big hug or pat on the back and tell yourself you can do it!... Remember it's the rational thought that counts! ...

Plus, I am going to give you the following cheat sheet that I've used many, many times myself. It works really well—so well, in fact, you will likely find, after asking yourself a couple of the cheat sheet questions listed on the following pages, that you can automatically come up with an alternative, rational thought to replace the counterproductive thought! You don't have to complete all the questions listed on the cheat sheet; choose the ones that seem to fit for your particular counterproductive thought. Remember, it's the rational thought that counts! ☙

Your Very Own Cheat Sheet!

Starting from the top, ask yourself one question at a time. Try to come up with an alternative thought to challenge your counterproductive thinking error. Some of the questions may not apply to your particular case. If so, just move on to the next one. See the examples below called Veronica's Cheat Sheet Responses and Ian's Cheat Sheet Responses.

What counterproductive thought do I want to challenge right now?

_____

_____

_____

_____

Is it true? If not, why not?

_____

_____

_____

_____

Can I prove it?

_____

_____

_____

_____

How do I know?

_____

_____

_____

_____

What category does this counterproductive thought fit into?

_____

Why does it fit this category?

_____
_____
_____

Why is it misguided for me to think this way?

_____
_____
_____

How would I talk a friend out of such an idea?

_____
_____
_____
_____

What would happen if _____?

_____
_____
_____
_____
_____
_____
_____

If that's true, what's the worst thing that can happen?

_____

_____

_____

_____

_____

_____

So what if that happens?

_____

_____

_____

_____

_____

_____

How would that be so terrible?

_____

_____

_____

_____

_____

_____

Where's the evidence?

_____

_____

_____

_____

_____

_____

Ask yourself: Can I still find happiness?

_____

_____

_____

What good things can happen if _____ occurs?

_____

_____

_____

_____

_____

_____

What good things might happen if _____does not occur?

_____

_____

_____

_____

_____

_____

_____

Can I be happy even if I don't get what I want?

_____

_____

_____

_____

_____

What might happen?

_____

_____

_____

_____

_____

_____

How terrible would that be?

_____

_____

_____

_____

_____

Why would this devastate me?

_____

_____

_____

_____

_____

What is the probability of a bad consequence?

_____

_____

_____

_____

_____

_____

What percentage of time has _____ actually been proven correct?

_____

_____

_____

_____

What is my new alternative (productive) belief?

_____

_____

_____

_____

_____

_____

_____

How does my new alternative (productive) belief make me feel?

_____

_____

_____

_____

_____

_____

How am I likely going to behave about this situation/circumstance given my new positive way of thinking and feeling?

_____

_____

_____

_____

_____

What will the likely consequence(s) be as a result?

_____

_____

_____

_____

_____

_____

_____

Other comments?

_____

_____

_____

_____

_____

_____

_____

_____

_____

_____

_____

_____

_____

_____

_____

_____

_____

Example of Veronica's Cheat Sheet Responses

What counterproductive thought do I want to challenge right now?

I'm a bad parent.

Is it true? If not, why not? I guess that thought isn't really true. I'm not ALL bad.

Can I prove it?

No, I really can't prove that I'm all bad.

How do I know?

Because I've been very involved in Kate's life.

What category does this counterproductive thought fit into?

It's all-or-nothing thinking and a mental filter.

Why does it fit this category?

I'm being black and white and only dwelling on the negatives. I'm ignoring the positives.

Why is it misguided for me to think this way?

I'm putting myself down and my self-esteem is low enough already. Saying I'm a bad parent is not a good term to use

How would I talk a friend out of such an idea?

That would be fairly easy to do. I'd give her examples of ways she's proven to be a wonderful mother to her children.

What would happen if _____?

If there were ways to prove to myself that I'm truly a bad parent, then I'd definitely want to work on making things different.

If that's true, what's the worst thing that can happen?

If I were a bad parent, then it's completely justifiable for Kate to not want to have anything to do with me possibly for the rest of my life. I would do anything it takes. I'd take parenting classes. And I'd get lots of therapy.

So what if that happens?

Seeing a therapist and taking parenting classes wouldn't be so bad. There are lots of things I could learn. Personal growth is always a positive thing.

How would that be so terrible?

It wouldn't be.

Where's the evidence?

There is no evidence.

Ask yourself: Can I still find happiness?

Yes, I can. I can be proud of who I am and respect my-self for who I am. I am a worthy person.

What good things can happen if _____ occurs?

What good things might happen if _____ does not occur?

Can I be happy even if I don't get what I want?

What might happen?

_____

_____

_____

_____

_____

How terrible would that be?

_____

_____

_____

_____

Why would this devastate me?

_____

_____

_____

_____

_____

_____

What is the probability of a bad consequence?

_____

_____

_____

_____

_____

_____

What percentage of time has _____ actually been proven correct?

_____

_____

_____

_____

What is my new alternative (productive) belief?

I am a kind, concerned, thoughtful, warm, caring and
loving parent. I can be proud of and respect myself.
I am a worthy person. It's natural for parents to
make mistakes. I learn from mistakes.

_____

_____

_____

How does my new alternative (productive) belief make me feel? _____

I feel better now. I fell more self—assured and self—
confident. I feel happier too.

_____

_____

_____

How am I likely going to behave about this situation/circumstance given my new
positive way of thinking and feeling?

I am going to do my best to be as positive as I can be
especially when Kate puts me down. I will do my best
not to react whenever she says I'm a bad parent. I'll
validate Kate's feelings and apologize for mistakes
made.

What will the likely consequence(s) be as a result?

My self-confidence and self-esteem will continue to increase.

Other comments?

Example of Ian's Cheat Sheet Responses

What counterproductive thought do I want to challenge right now?

The attorneys and judge will think I'm an idiot if they see my hands shaking during the trial.

Is it true? If not, why not? *No, it's not true because lots of people normally experience anxiety including hand shaking while standing in front of a judge and others. That doesn't make them idiots though.*

Can I prove it?

No.

How do I know?

I really don't know.

What category does this counterproductive thought fit into?

Mind reading

Why does it fit this category?

Because I'm making a negative assumption about what I think they'll be thinking about me.

Why is it misguided for me to think this way? *When I've seen other people's hands shake, I don't think they're idiots.*

How would I talk a friend out of such an idea?

I'd tell my friend it's quite natural to feel anxious during a trial. So what if your hands shake. It's not very likely they'll notice the shaking and even so that isn't a sign of being an idiot. Your assumption is probably exaggerated.

What would happen if _____?

If my hands shake during the trial nobody will notice, only one or two of them may notice, perhaps the three of them notice, or maybe everyone in the courtroom will notice.

If that's true, what's the worst thing that can happen?

Nothing! It won't be the end of the world.

So what if that happens?

Any person who may notice that my hands are shaking will think I'm feeling a little anxious.

How would that be so terrible?

It wouldn't be so terrible!

Where's the evidence?

It's normal to experience hand shaking sometimes. The judge and attorneys will likely think nothing of it if they even notice it.

Ask yourself: Can I still find happiness?

Yes, because I won't let any sign of anxiety prevent me from leading a full and happy life.

What good things can happen if _____ occurs?

If my hands begin to shake I can practice breathing better and relax. Then I'll be focused and do the best I can.

What good things might happen if _____ does not occur?

If my hands don't shake at all, I'll still be focused and do the best I can.

Can I be happy even if I don't get what I want?

Yes, I can be happy. I just need to do the very best I can given the circumstances. A little anxiety can be a good thing.

What might happen?

I honestly don't know and don't plan on making any assumptions.

How terrible would that be?

I can't answer this question.

Why would this devastate me?

I can't answer this question either.

What is the probability of a bad consequence?

The probability of a bad consequence such as hand shaking isn't too high.

What percentage of time has _____ actually been proven correct?

Probably less than 10 % of the time I've experienced hand shaking when anxious.

What is my new alternative (productive) belief?

Some people in the courtroom may notice my hands shaking but it's unlikely that they will believe I'm an idiot.

How does my new alternative (productive) belief make me feel? _____

I feel much better.

How am I likely going to behave about this situation/circumstance given my new positive way of thinking and feeling?

I'll cope just fine because there is a lot of evidence to demonstrate that PAS is occurring. I'll be able to focus on my breathing, stand tall and look self-confident.

_____

_____

What will the likely consequence(s) be as a result?

I'll stay focused, listen well and be able to prove

my case.

_____

_____

_____

_____

Other comments?

_____

_____

_____

_____

_____

_____

_____

_____

_____

_____

_____

_____

_____

_____

_____

Chapter Fourteen
Coping with Grief and Loss

Trying to ignore your pain or keep it from surfacing will only make it worse and prolong the grief process. It is absolutely necessary to confront your grief and actively process it.

Throughout our lives we are faced with significant losses and must cope with grief. The effects of PAS are no exception. The loss of a once loved partner, a marriage, an intact family unit, a shared family home, selling your family home, loss of financial stability, perhaps loss of health, loss of friendships, loss of cherished dreams, to name a few. The losses, combined with the effects of undergoing the dynamics of PAS, mark the beginning of one of the most painful times in an alienated parent's life. That painful beginning whereby one's life seems to be turned upside down is the first step on a long and winding road to a sense of wholeness. There is no normal timetable for grieving. On average, however, it takes most individuals two or more years of recovery through grief. With severe cases of PAS, the grief process can take much longer.

... The losses, combined with the effects of undergoing the dynamics of PAS, mark the beginning of one of the most painful times in an alienated parent's life...

Although an alienated parent will grieve in his or her own unique way, how one grieves is based on varying factors including one's personality and coping style, his/her life experiences, his/her faith, and the nature of the alienation. Trying to ignore your pain or keep it from surfacing will only make it worse and prolong the grief process. It is absolutely necessary to confront your grief and actively process it. Please remember: feeling sad, lonely, frightened, and angry are normal reactions to loss. It's healthy to cry. Crying doesn't mean you're a weak or fragile person. Don't try to protect yourself, your family, or friends by putting on a brave face. Showing your true inner feelings can help them and you.

The traditional model of grieving (Kübler-Ross, 1969) consists of five stages:

Shock and Denial:

"I'm so confused and feel so numb."

"No, you're wrong. What do you mean I'm no good or a bad parent?"

"This can't be happening to me. I've had such a good relationship with my kids."

Anger:

"Why on earth is this happening? My ex is all to blame for this. He has poisoned my children with lies."

"I feel so frustrated, annoyed, and such shame."

Bargaining:

"I'll do whatever it takes to not let this happen. In return I will _____."

"God, I promise to pray to you every single day. I won't forget ever again. Please, I pray that my daughter will talk to me again."

"Just let me see my children. I'll do anything."

Depression:

"I feel so sad and let down."

"Why bother going on. I'll never see my son again."

"What's the point in trying? He's totally programmed my kids against me."

... The traditional model of grieving (Kübler-Ross, 1969) consists of five stages ...

Acceptance:

"I can't change what's happened but I can do my best in handling the circumstances."

"I'm at peace with what has happened. I can and will get through this."

"Learn to get in touch with the silence within yourself, and know that everything in life has purpose. There are no mistakes, no coincidences, all events are blessings given to us to learn from."

~ Dr. Elizabeth Kübler-Ross

... I can't change what's happened but I can do my best in handling the circumstances ...

Brendon's Sample Loss Chart

Relationships	Work or School	Money	Health	Other Important Things	Time
I feel very alone.	It's "Bring your Kids to Work Day" tomorrow. I'm such a loser.	The bitch has taken everything from me. I'm broke.	I'm so depressed.	I can't even think about dating right now.	I'm zoning out from watching too much sports on TV.
Jane divorced me.	I can't complete this semester of my MBA program.	I can't pay my bills.	I've gained so much weight from eating junk food.	I have no self-esteem.	I can't keep up with the bills.
My kids hate me.	I'm missing a lot of work these days.	The bank is harassing me.	I started smoking again.	I can't afford a gym membership anymore.	I'm in my head too much.
My in-laws won't have anything to do with me anymore.	My boss is pissed off with me.	I can't renew my mortgage because Jane won't sign the papers.	Who'd ever want to date me because I've gained so much weight.	My ex still has a gym membership there.	I spend so much time talking to my lawyer.
My brother- and sister-in-law won't talk to me. We used to be so close.	I didn't get my annual raise.	I can't believe all those years I contributed to a spousal RSP. It's upsetting that she gets to keep it all.	I haven't slept through the night for over three months now.	I feel like my reputation is at stake here.	I don't have time to deal with any more crises.
I've shut myself off from my friends.	People keep asking me questions about why I haven't seen my children.	I can't afford to pay for a good lawyer.	I could barely afford health insurance prior to PAS. Now I can't at all.	I feel so hopeless.	Just one more and I'm totally going to crack.
My kids stopped wanting to see me last week.	Joe made fun of me today.	This court battle has sucked me dry.	I'm anxious. It's court tomorrow.	This isn't fair.	Missed not being able to go to the school Christmas concert.
I feel even more alone now.	I didn't get a promotion.	I can hardly pay my rent.	Nail biting.	Miss my old house. This place is crap.	Will time ever heal my pain?
I miss my dog Sam who lives with Jane and our children.	I can't concentrate at work.	How will I be able to buy a birthday present for Kyle? He's turning 7.	I've seen my doctor more than I've seen my children.	Found out that Kyle never got the little gift I bought him. Jane didn't give it to him.	Lost years not being around the children.

Exercise: My Losses—Consider all of the losses you have experienced since PAS began. See the prior example on how Brendon filled out his own loss chart.

Relationships	Work or School	Money	Health	Other Important Things	Time

Five Tips on How to Deal with the Loss of not
Seeing Your Child or Children

Confront your loss

Confront your loss. Talk about it. Share it with supportive people including your therapist, friends, and relatives. Talk about what happened, why you think it happened, when it happened, where it happened, how you're dealing with all this, and so on. Validate it.

Sit in a quiet space that you find peaceful and relaxing

Sit in a quiet space that you find peaceful and relaxing. Recall fond memories and stories of being with your family prior to PAS occurring. What were some of the fun things you and your family did together? What were some of the special things you did together? What peculiar or quirky things did you used to do? What's the earliest positive recollection you have of your child/children?

Put together a treasure box

Put together a treasure box full of photographs, letters, cards, toys, and/or any collectibles that symbolize your relationship with your child/children. Not only can your treasure box help you recall fond memories of being with your children and help integrate the grief, but it can also help your children upon potential reunification to recognize and acknowledge that you have never forgotten about them. One word of caution, however; one of the risks of putting a treasure box together and spending time going through the various collectibles from time to time is it may prevent you from noticing all the positive things that life has to offer. It would not be healthy for you to choose to single-mindedly focus on the losses.

... Talk about what happened, why you think it happened, when it happened, where it happened, how you're dealing with all this, and so on. Validate it ...

When you start blaming yourself

When you start blaming yourself or feeling guilty, then offer yourself some reassurance. Remind yourself that you cannot be completely responsible for the demise of your relationship with your children. Remind yourself that your children have been programmed to alienate you. Remind yourself that this is not your children's fault either. Remind yourself that you have been and will always continue to be a loving parent. Trust yourself and your instincts.

Remember

Remember that there is no such thing as a super parent. Please just do what you can, when you can, and be gentle on yourself. Accept that some things just can't be made better in a short period of time. Trust yourself that you will survive. ❧

...When you start blaming yourself or feeling guilty, then offer yourself some reassurance. Remind yourself that you cannot be completely responsible for the demise of your relationship with your children ...

Chapter Fifteen
How to Rise Above the Stress

Stress is something that each and every one of us faces on a daily basis, some more than others. We all need a certain amount of stress in our lives to remain alive.

Stress is something that each and every one of us faces on a daily basis, some more than others. We all need a certain amount of stress in our lives to remain alive. Quite simply, the stress response is a natural physical reaction to the perception that we are experiencing some type of threat. Consequently, stress is inevitable when you're being alienated by your former spouse and family. Having the ability to rise above this stress first requires a greater understanding of the nature of stress.

... stress is inevitable when you're being alienated by your former spouse and family. Having the ability to rise above this stress first requires a greater understanding of the nature of stress ...

What is so fascinating from both physiological and psychological viewpoints is that most individuals feel less able to cope when the stress response is triggered. So why is that? From an evolutionary perspective, the answer is that the stress response developed millions of years ago when the greatest threats to well-being involved violent life-or-death situations. Back then, as a hunter or a gatherer, you might have been attacked and killed by a large predator in the bush; or, you might have been attacked by another tribe in the jungle when you least expected it. Your greatest odds for survival likely involved one of two choices: fight as hard as you possibly could, or run away as fast as you possibly could. There's a risk that you would not have survived if you chose to do nothing. That is why the stress response is also called the fight, flight (run), or freeze (do nothing) response. You may have heard of the term "survival of the fittest" meaning that those who fought the hardest or ran the fastest were more likely to live and to pass along their characteristics to their offspring (Darwin). Therefore, the trigger for the stress response to be activated is a belief or perception that we are under some type of threat or endangerment whether real or imagined.

Numerous physiological changes take place when you perceive a threat and your stress response is activated. They are:

- Increased heart rate to help pump blood more efficiently to your working muscles.

- Increased pulse rate and heart pounding.

- Increased respiration to get additional oxygen from the environment.

- Increased blood sugar levels due to the release of glucose from your liver.

- Increased blood supply to your large muscles through the widening of blood vessels in those areas.

- Decreased blood supply to your digestive system and skin through the narrowing of blood vessels in those areas.

- Increased flood of stress hormones, including adrenaline and cortisol, are released into the bloodstream.

- Immune and sexual functions are suppressed.

And much more!

Additionally, numerous emotional and behavioral changes occur during the stress response. They are:

- The stress response makes you feel alert.

- The stress response helps you stay focused.

- The stress response helps you stay energetic.

- The stress response gives you extra strength to defend yourself.

... the trigger for the stress response to be activated is a belief or perception that we are under some type of threat or endangerment whether real or imagined ...

- The stress response helps you rise to meet various challenges.

- The stress response helps keep you on your toes.

- The stress response helps sharpen your concentration.

- The stress response can literally help save your life.

- The stress response can voluntarily suppress your emotions.

- The stress response can trigger fear and negativity.

And much more!

Long-term exposure to stress can lead to serious health conditions including, but not limited to, high blood pressure, heart attacks, heart disease, strokes, infertility, digestive problems, sleep difficulties, obesity, autoimmune diseases, certain types of cancers, skin conditions, increase of the aging process, anxiety disorders, depression, and various types of pain throughout the body.

... Due to the widespread damage stress can cause, it's important to recognize what your own limits are. Just how much stress is considered too much actually differs from one person to another ...

The types of pressures that you experience in the here and now are real. Due to the widespread damage stress can cause, it's important to recognize what your own limits are. Just how much stress is considered too much actually differs from one person to another. Some individuals can roll with the punches while others will fall apart at the slightest annoyance. Still others seem to thrive on the challenge and excitement of a high-stress environment. Your ability to tolerate stress as an alienated parent will depend on many factors.

Take a few moments to consider the types of obstacles and/or pressures you are currently facing on a regular basis.

Time for Self-Reflection

Write down one of the situations in which you felt yourself becoming stressed in the past week.

_____

_____

_____

_____

_____

_____

_____

Besides feeling stressed, what other feelings did you experience at the time?

_____

_____

_____

_____

_____

_____

Can you recall feeling like your life was out of control? Or you were out of control?

_____

_____

_____

_____

_____

_____

_____

_____

Can you recall wanting to escape the situation?

_____

_____

_____

_____

_____

_____

_____

Can you recall wanting to run away and/or scream really loud to help cope with this situation?

_____

_____

_____

_____

_____

_____

Can you recall wanting to attack someone verbally, emotionally, and/or physically? For example, phone your former spouse and chew him/her out for not letting you see your child during your court-mandated visiting time.

_____

_____

_____

_____

_____

_____

_____

What would the likely consequences be of those particular actions?

_____

_____

_____

_____

_____

_____

_____

_____

_____

Were you able to rise above the stress? If so, what did you do?

_____

_____

_____

_____

_____

_____

_____

_____

_____

_____

_____

_____

Give yourself another great big pat on the back or hug yourself!

Strategies for Alienated Parents to Rise Above the Stress

Build a Strong Network

Build a strong network of supportive friends and family members to act as a buffer against the stressors in your life. Do your very best not to isolate yourself and feel lonely. The greater the loneliness and isolation you experience, the greater you will be vulnerable to more stress.

Increase Your Sense of Control

Increase your sense of control. Given that alienated parents are highly vulnerable to stress, it's not uncommon to feel like things are out of control. At a time like this, it's important that you have confidence in yourself and your ability to be able to influence certain situations or events. Have enough self-confidence to recognize that you can and will persevere through the obstacles and challenges in your life. Believe in yourself! Believe in your children's best interests! They need you in their lives.

Do Regular Check-ins on Your Attitude and Outlook

... Do regular check-ins on your attitude and outlook. It's important to maintain an optimistic attitude. Accept that none of us can have complete control over what happens in our lives. Embrace the challenges and changes that have taken place ...

Do regular check-ins on your attitude and outlook. It's important to maintain an optimistic attitude. Accept that none of us can have complete control over what happens in our lives. Embrace the challenges and changes that have taken place. Accept that change is a part of life. Consider whether or not you are looking at your personal situation in a positive light and with a positive attitude. Be aware of how many times per day you think or say negative things about yourself, your ex, your children, or others. Ensure you have a good sense of humor. Laughter truly can be one of your best prescriptions for coping purposes. Consider embracing some form of spirituality, whether it means believing in a higher power, the cosmos, or having a sense of purpose in life.

Do Regular Check-ins on Your Emotions

Do regular check-ins on your emotions. Alienated parents are extremely vulnerable to stress when they don't know how to deal with their feelings. Suppressing your feelings isn't healthy, nor is getting extremely agitated, angry, and doing something foolish. Learn how to calm and soothe yourself whenever you're feeling sad, mad, frustrated, betrayed, afraid, or angry. You can make healthy choices. Remember, it's not what you have, it's what you do with what you have. You truly have the ability to bring your emotions into balance. In doing so, it will help you bounce back from adversity. Ask yourself, "Am I in control of my stress or is my stress in control of me?"

Be Knowledgeable and Prepared

Be knowledgeable and prepared. The more knowledge you have about a potential stressful situation, including how long it will likely last and what to expect, the easier it will be for you to cope. For example, if you go to court with a realistic picture of what to expect when your former spouse's attorney claims you physically abused your oldest daughter during your last visit and you did no such thing, then have a valid argument prepared for the judge. Then there's a much greater chance that the judge will recognize that PAS is occurring.

... The more knowledge you have about a potential stressful situation, including how long it will likely last and what to expect, the easier it will be for you to cope ...

Give Yourself an Energy Boost

Give yourself an energy boost through eating healthy, nutritious meals on a regular and consistent basis.

Engage in Regular Exercise

Engage in regular exercise. Studies show that individuals who participate in regular aerobic or anaerobic exercise often reveal less stress and anxiety than those who don't (Hays, 1999). Choose a variety of physical activities and recreational activities that you enjoy or will at least tolerate! Three to four times a week is best. Don't overdo it and if you haven't exercised for some time, start by enjoying regular walks and slowly increasing your pace. You will notice the physical and psychological benefits of engaging in regular exercise quite quickly.

Keep Your Caffeine Intake at a Minimum

Keep your caffeine intake at a minimum. Although caffeine, coffee in particular, may help you feel more alert and help to carry you through difficult days, it stimulates your nervous system. Additionally, caffeine is hidden in numerous products including colas and other soft drinks; black, green, or other teas; decaf coffee; dark and milk chocolate; foods containing chocolate such as chocolate ice-cream; energy drinks; certain herbal stimulants; certain prescribed medications; certain over-the-counter drugstore items; and coffee-flavored foods such as coffee yogurt and iced coffee-flavored drinks. Any type of caffeine will block your adenosine neurotransmitters, which are what promote sleep. Too much caffeine in our systems results in sleep problems, restlessness, irritability, nervousness, exhaustion, muscle tremors/jitters, nausea, heartburn, increased or irregular heart rate, dehydration and thirstiness, and addiction.

... Keep your caffeine intake at a minimum. Although caffeine, coffee in particular, may help you feel more alert and help to carry you through difficult days, it stimulates your nervous system ...

Learn to Breathe Effectively

Learn to breathe effectively. A recommended breathing strategy is provided in chapter 16.

Practice Other Relaxation Strategies Often

Practice other relaxation strategies often: mindfulness, meditation, yoga, progressive muscle relaxation, or guided imagery. See chapter 16 for more information.

Watch your Alcohol Consumption and Any Other Substance Use

Watch your alcohol consumption and any other substance use—tobacco, prescription drug use, or any illicit drug use. It might seem like a good idea to have a drink, a smoke, or a toke to cope, relax, sleep, but drug and alcohol misuse can easily turn into abuse and dependence for some individuals. This is especially true if there is a family history of addiction. It's important to become self-educated on the immediate, short-term, and long-term effects of any substance. In the event that you or someone else who cares about you believes that you have a problem, it's important to seek help as soon as possible. Talk to your physician or a mental health professional.

Watch for Any Other Patterns of Addictive Behaviors

Watch for any other patterns of addictive behaviors. Besides being cautious about engaging in any type of mind-altering addictive behaviors such as drinking and drugging, watch out for mood-altering addictive behaviors, too. Problem gambling, sexual acting out, compulsive spending and over-spending, compulsive shopping, disordered eating, and ongoing codependency in relationships are all examples of mood-altering addictive behaviors. If you easily become thrilled by any of the aforementioned mood-altering addictive behaviors, talk to your physician or a mental health professional as soon as possible.

... Watch your alcohol consumption and any other substance use—tobacco, prescription drug use, or any illicit drug use. It might seem like a good idea to have a drink, a smoke, or a toke to cope, relax, sleep, but drug and alcohol misuse can easily turn into abuse and dependence for some individuals ...

Engage in a Regular Sleep Pattern

Engage in a regular sleep pattern. Recent surveys conducted by the National Sleep Foundation (2005) showed that at least forty million Americans suffer from varying sleep disorders. Stress is the number one reason for short-term sleep problems. By engaging in a regular sleep/wake cycle daily, you will feel more alert, refreshed, and energized, among other things. In the event that you are experiencing sleep disturbances, consult with your physician or a mental health professional.

Journal Daily

I urge you to use a journal daily to write out your thoughts and feelings. Also, journals are very important to keep track of various situations or events that take place between you, your former spouse, your children, the criminal justice system, and so on. If deemed appropriate, share your journal entries with your attorney for legal purposes.

Blog

... I have encouraged many alienated parents to consider blogging their stories about family alienation online. One benefit of blogging is finding out that you're not in an isolated situation ...

One of the benefits of social media is the ability to blog. Many bloggers sell products, network with others who share the same profession, use blogging for job searches, and so on. Blogging has also become a popular way to post online journals and diaries. I have encouraged many alienated parents to consider blogging their stories about family alienation online. One benefit of blogging is finding out that you're not in an isolated situation. Additionally, blogging offers the ability for you to meet other individuals who will offer you support just as you may to them. Many alienated parents have reported that it's validating to blog because there are so many other parents out there who comment on understanding the profound pain of losing a child through parental alienation. In some cases, I've also seen alienated children reconnect with their alienated parents from reading their parents' blogs.

Join a PAS Online Support Group

Join a PAS online support group or an in-person support group if one is available in your area. The International Network of Alienated Families, for instance, is a support group located in Southern California that provides monthly group meetings and is facilitated by mental health professionals who are experienced with PA and PAS. If there isn't an existing support group in your area, why not consider starting one? This can be easily accomplished through Meetup, http://www.meetup.com. Another option is to join a PAS online support group and organization. Here are some examples:

- The **PAS Guardian Angels**, a support group for parents who have lost contact with their children due to PAS located at: http://groups.yahoo.com/group/PAS-GuardianAngels.

- The **Experience Project** hosts a support group for PAS families at http://www.experienceproject.com/groups/Lost-My-Children-To-Parental-Alienation/160766.

- **Keeping Families Connected** offers resources to identify, battle, and recover from Parental Alienation: http://www.keepingfamiliesconnected.org.

- **Lee PAS Foundation** is dedicated to bringing awareness and education of Parental Alienation and parental kidnap to the public: http://www.leepasfoundation.org.

- **Parental Alienation and Hostile Aggressive Parenting Awareness** contains helpful information for parents and professionals: http://www.paawareness.com.

- **The Rachel Foundation for Family Integration** provides reintegration services for parents and children whose bonds of love and affection have been damaged or destroyed by abduction and/or alienation: http://www.rachelfoundation.org.

- **Children Need Both Parents** is a non-profit organization promoting both parents in the lives of children: http://www.cnbpinc.org.

... If there isn't an existing support group in your area, why not consider starting one? ...

• **Children's Rights Council (CRC)** works to assure a child has frequent, meaningful, and regular contact with parents and extended family after divorce or separation: http://www.crckids.org.

• **Coalition for Equal Parenting** is a gender-neutral, non-profit organization that promotes equality for all parties of divorce and advocates on behalf of parents who have been impacted by Parental Alienation: http://www.coalitionforequalparenting. org.

• **DadsDivorce.com** carries essential information and resources for fathers at any stage of divorce: http://dadsdivorce.com.

• **DivorceMagazine.com** provides information and advice about divorce law, divorce lawyers, family law, children and divorce, and other divorce-related issues. The site also carries excerpts of A Family's Heartbreak: A Parent's Introduction to Parental Alienation at: http://www.divorcemag.com/articles/Parental-Alienation-Syndrome.

... an organization dedicated to a child's fundamental right to be loved, guided, nurtured, and educated by both fit and willing parents ...

• **Divorce Recovery Suite** is a user-friendly family law site providing a chat room, information on state statutes, and a collection of links regarding divorce, law, forms, rights, and healing: http://www.divorcerecoverysuite.com.

• **Families Need Fathers** seeks to obtain the best possible blend of both parents in the lives of children: http://www.fnf.org.uk.

• **Jewish Unity for Multiple Parenting (JUMP)** campaigns for improved relationships between divorced parents and their children in the Jewish community: http://pa-pa.org/index.php?option=com_wrapper&view=wrapper&Itemid=157.

- **A Child's Right** is an organization dedicated to a child's fundamental right to be loved, guided, nurtured, and educated by both fit and willing parents: http://www.achildsright.typepad.com.

- **A Family's Heartbreak Facebook Page** is a social networking page designed to connect people struggling with Parental Alienation: http://www.facebook.com/#!/group.php?gid=61789494087&ref=ts.

- **Parental Alienation Global Directory and Resource Services** contains very good resources for alienated parents, families, and professionals: http://padirectory.info.

- **Parental Alienation Awareness Organization (PAAO)** offers tremendous resources for alienated families and professionals: http://www.paawareness.org.

Balance your life

The key to functioning as effectively as you can during this very difficult and painful time is to do your best to experience a balanced lifestyle. Myers, Sweeney, and Witmer's (2000) model of wellness is useful to keep in mind. Their model focuses on five life tasks: essence or spirituality, work and leisure, friendship, love, and self-direction; and twelve sub tasks: sense of worth, sense of control, realistic beliefs, emotional awareness and coping, problem solving and creativity, sense of humor, nutrition, exercise, self-care, stress management, gender identity, and cultural identity. Folks who utilize this model of wellness will experience more health and wellness than those who choose not to.

... If all else fails, please seek counseling from a well-qualified mental health professional who is experienced in working with alienated parents ...

If all else fails, please seek counseling from a well-qualified mental health professional who is experienced in working with alienated parents. ❧

Time for Self-Reflection

Which of the above strategies have you recently used to help rise above the stress? _____

_____

_____

_____

_____

_____

_____

_____

_____

_____

_____

_____

_____

_____

Which of the above strategies have you not used for a long time or perhaps never tried before?

_____

_____

_____

_____

_____

_____

_____

_____

_____

_____

_____

_____

If you were to pick three of the above strategies to engage in within the next week, what would they be?

_____

_____

_____

_____

_____

_____

_____

_____

_____

_____

On a self-estimated scale of 0-10 (0 = I have no desire and don't plan to engage in any of the above-noted strategies to help rise above the stress, 10 = I have the utmost desire and nothing is going to stop me from engaging in at least three of the strategies I chose above), which number would you pick? Give reasons for why you chose that number on your scale.

_____

_____

_____

_____

_____

_____

_____

_____

_____

_____

_____

_____

Think of some kind of reward you can easily give yourself after achieving at least three of the above-noted strategies to help rise above the stress. Choose a reward that may not necessarily cost any money, is something you really like or enjoy, and is healthy for you. For example, your reward at the end of the week after achieving at least three stress management strategies may be taking a bubble bath, giving yourself a big hug, eating your favorite kind of apple, going hiking at your favorite spot, and so forth. What will your reward be?

_____

_____

_____

_____

_____

_____

_____

_____

_____

_____

_____

_____

_____

_____

_____

_____

_____

_____

_____

_____

_____

_____

_____

_____

Chapter Sixteen
How to Behave Your Way out of Things You Fear

Each and every one of us experiences fear and anxiety from time to time—some people more than others. Alienated parents are not excluded by any means. This chapter will provide you effective strategies to help you behave your way out of things that may elicit fear and anxiety throughout the difficult trajectory of PAS.

The terms fear and anxiety have been loosely considered the same thing in popular culture. For the sake of a common working definition, let's make use of the definitions of Beck and Emery (1985). According to them, fear is defined as a cognitive assessment of a threatening stimulus whereas anxiety is an emotional reaction to that assessment. Each and every one of us experiences fear and anxiety from time to time—some people more than others. Alienated parents are not excluded by any means. This chapter will provide you some effective strategies to help you behave your way out of things that may elicit fear and anxiety throughout the difficult trajectory of PAS.

...When feeling anxious or frightened about something, it's easy to forget to breathe naturally and easily. In some cases, we can hyperventilate or hypo-ventilate, sometimes mild panic ensues, or a person may even experience a full-blown panic attack ...

The 1-4 Breath and Distress Measurement Method:

You have probably heard others say, "Just breathe!" When feeling anxious or frightened about something, it's easy to forget to breathe naturally and easily. In some cases, we can hyperventilate or hypo-ventilate, sometimes mild panic ensues, or a person may even experience a full-blown panic attack. The 1-4 Breath Technique is terrific for releasing fear, anxiety, nervousness, anger, or any strong emotion because it balances our sympathetic and parasympathetic nervous systems in our bodies. You can use it anywhere at any time. I've used it many times myself when having to act as a witness or expert witness in court. You will likely find it's best to do this breathing technique by inhaling and exhaling through your nose. However, if that's not possible, don't let that stop you from breathing through your mouth.

Step 1:

First measure yourself on a scale of 0 – 10 (0 = I'm not experiencing any distress, 5 = I'm experiencing medium distress, and 10 = I'm experiencing the most distress imaginable), pick a number on the incremental scale between 0 –10 that best describes what you are feeling right now.

For example: *"Right now, I'm a 7."*

Step 2:

Inhale to the count of four seconds, hold your breath for four seconds, and then exhale for four seconds. Do this cycle four times in a row.

Step 3:

Reassess your level of distress on a scale of 0-10. It's likely that your level of distress has decreased by at least one increment on the scale. Continue the breathing exercise until distress is gone.

Progressive Muscle Relaxation:

There are lots of ways to experience the wonders of progressive muscle relaxation (PMR), for example, PMR CDs and DVDs. As of this printing Amazon.com shows several MP3 downloads for as little as a dollar. Alternatively, find a good book online or at your local bookstore that contains a PMR script that you can use on your own or with a partner. PMR is a great way to alleviate stress and other strong emotions. To me, it's like going to the spa and having a great massage without having to book an appointment and paying a lot of money for it!

... PMR is a great way to alleviate stress and other strong emotions. To me, it's like going to the spa and having a great massage without having to book an appointment and paying a lot of money for it! ...

Stop Technique:

The Stop Technique is very helpful for times when your mind starts racing, worrying, or ruminating. It's very simple too. Here's all you need to do. Whenever racing thoughts or worries begin, say to yourself, "Stop! These thoughts are not healthy or helpful for me right now and this is not my scheduled racing or worry time." You may need to repeat this over and over again in your mind (or out loud if you're in a private space) until your mind becomes conditioned to this technique. It's best to use this particular technique in conjunction with the next technique—schedule worry time.

Schedule Worry Time:

As previously mentioned, use this technique alongside the Stop Technique. Write down your racing thoughts and worries in a regular notebook, a journal, or the notes section of your electronic device. In doing so, it's impossible to forget your worries! Then you can put those worries aside for the time being. Once written down, you're not allowed to worry about them.

... Each day set aside ten to fifteen minutes, once in the morning and once in the mid afternoon to early evening. This will be your very own scheduled worry time ...

Each day set aside ten to fifteen minutes, once in the morning and once in the mid afternoon to early evening. This will be your very own scheduled worry time. If possible, use a timer so you don't exceed the ten to fifteen minutes of scheduled worry time. During this time, pull out your list of worries and worry to your heart's content. Once the timer goes off or the time has elapsed though, stop worrying because your time is up.

Visualization:

This technique is highly recommended to help overcome stress, anxiety, fear, and other strong emotions. The interesting thing is that it really does work and you may also end up smiling!

Find a comfortable place to sit or lie down. Close your eyes and picture yourself in a place that feels safe, calm, peaceful, tranquil, and serene. Perhaps it's a place you've been to for a vacation, your childhood cottage by a lake, a beautiful garden, or your favorite hiking trail. Your calm place can be virtually anywhere you want.

It can be real or imagined—as long as it will help to conjure up feelings of relaxation, peacefulness, and happiness. Practice your visualization exercise for five minutes each time.

Mindfulness:

Mindfulness is also called present moment awareness, which is the opposite of distraction. This technique helps your mind become calm and focused while your body becomes relaxed. It's recommended that you practice mindfulness daily for at least five minutes at a time. Skill learning will come with practice. Choose at least one activity daily to practice mindfulness. For example, if you are out on a leisurely or brisk walk, walk mindfully and resist the urge to solve a problem or worry. Instead, absorb yourself in the feel of your shoes touching the pavement, the sounds of birds chirping, the blowing wind and the rustle of the trees, the sound of the waves crashing, and so on. Put up some signs or posters around your home or office to serve as reminders. The practice is relatively easy, but remembering to practice can be the real challenge!

... Choose at least one activity daily to practice mindfulness. For example, if you are out on a leisurely or brisk walk, walk mindfully and resist the urge to solve a problem or worry ...

Meditation:

Similar to PMR, there are numerous sources available to help you learn to relax and improve your overall well-being through the process of meditation. You can join a meditation group, purchase meditation CDs or DVDs, practice it solely, join a yoga group, etc. It's a good idea to become familiar with the various types of meditation and pick one that fits comfortably for you. It's like trying out a new pair of jeans. Some fit better than others! ☙

Time for Self-Reflection

What techniques listed in this chapter have you used in the past? Were they helpful or not?

_____

_____

_____

_____

_____

_____

_____

_____

If they were helpful and you haven't been using them recently, ask yourself why not?

_____

_____

_____

_____

_____

_____

_____

_____

_____

_____

_____

_____

Are there any techniques listed in this chapter that you have never tried and are willing to consider trying? If yes, please describe. If no, ask yourself why not?

_____

_____

_____

_____

_____

_____

_____

_____

_____

_____

_____

Are there any techniques you have used, both past and present, that are not listed in this chapter that you have found helpful? Please describe.

_____

_____

_____

_____

_____

_____

_____

_____

_____

_____

_____

Chapter Seventeen
Watch Yourself

Whenever we make sacrifices, we place certain expectations upon ourselves as well as upon others. When those expectations are not met for whatever reasons, then we feel let down. The more let down we feel by unmet expectations, the more our own personal bitterness bank gets filled. Sooner or later our bitterness bank overflows with deposits. That's when anger ensues.

As you probably have noticed so far, PAS is a very complex issue. In true PAS cases, alienated parents are never prepared for it. How can one be? It's impossible. You're having a good, loving relationship with your child and then suddenly you're not. Your child may even experience a love-hate relationship with you almost overnight dependent upon how quickly they become programmed to alienate you.

...Whenever we make sacrifices, we place certain expectations upon ourselves as well as upon others. When those expectations are not met for whatever reasons, then we feel let down ...

Consider the following points. No matter where you stand at present in terms of the separation, divorce, or post-divorce process, just think of all the sacrifices you have made since you and your partner separated. Hopefully, you've had the opportunity to reflect on the material in Chapter Fourteen—Coping With Grief and Loss. You will likely feel surprised when you add up all of the sacrifices you have made.

Now, consider this. Whenever we make sacrifices, we place certain expectations upon ourselves as well as upon others. When those expectations are not met for whatever reasons, then we feel let down. The more let down we feel by unmet expectations, the more our own personal bitterness bank gets filled. Sooner or later our bitterness bank overflows with deposits. That's when anger ensues. And what happens then? Sometimes we intentionally set out to punish the other person, but generally speaking, we unconsciously or unknowingly do so. There are many different ways to punish a former partner. For example, we might retaliate, seek revenge, or plot to regain control.

Of course, the alienating parent is engaging in a lot of punishing behaviors against the target parent. Now, here is the clincher. Sometimes, the alienated parent can become very good at the above too, which leads to two-way or counter alienation.

Clearly, two-way or counter alienation is not okay. It's natural for an alienated parent to feel many of the negative emotions discussed in this book including frustration, anger, resentment, and betrayal. But, when the target parent gives in to the urge to seek revenge, his or her actions will ultimately backfire. The more a target parent chooses to engage in revenge-seeking behaviors, including badmouthing the other parent, the greater the likelihood of not being able to rekindle the broken relationship with the alienated children. It's definitely not worth trying even once.

There are numerous ways that an alienated parent can cope with all the negativity. Learning to challenge all of your negative thoughts and feelings will ultimately help you function in all aspects of life more effectively. In doing so, you will have a greater chance of rekindling your relationship with your alienated children. Additionally, there are numerous professional interventions available to help you along the way. Please remember, you're not alone. ✀

> *...two-way or counter alienation is not okay... when the target parent gives in to the urge to seek revenge, his or her actions will ultimately backfire....*

Time for Self-Reflection

After reading this short chapter, is there anything that you may need to watch out for? If so, briefly reflect on that here.

_____

_____

_____

_____

_____

_____

_____

_____

_____

_____

_____

_____

_____

_____

_____

Do you have any other comments regarding this chapter?

_____

_____

_____

_____

_____

_____

_____

_____

_____

Chapter Eighteen
Take Swift Action

The seeds of PAS can sprout quickly. Mild PAS in a child or youth can quickly progress into moderate and severe levels. As mentioned before, the greater the level of severity, the harder it is to reverse. It is absolutely necessary for an alienated parent to take swift action to help stop the progression and you're encouraged not to do this alone. Rather, please consider seeking professional assistance.

...Through the years, many alienated parents that I've seen in clinical practice have claimed the opposite. That is, they believed or had been advised by their friends, workmates, or family members, "Don't do anything—just let things happen naturally." ...

When I was a young girl my mother often said, "Don't just stand there. Do something!" And, so I did! I hope you will also consider my dear mother's advice because this saying holds a lot of truth and meaning when PA or PAS has been identified. The seeds of PAS can sprout quickly. Mild PAS in a child or youth can quickly progress into moderate and severe levels. As mentioned before, the greater the level of severity, the harder it is to reverse. It is absolutely necessary for an alienated parent to take swift action to help stop the progression and you're encouraged not to do this alone. Rather, please consider seeking professional assistance.

Through the years, many alienated parents that I've seen in clinical practice have claimed the opposite. That is, they believed or had been advised by their friends, workmates, or family members, "Don't do anything—just let things happen naturally." Many of these same parents were also under the impression that their alienated child or children would someday grow up and snap out of it. Unfortunately, for the most part, nothing can be further from the truth. Just as early detection of cancer can save lives, early detection of PA or PAS can save family relationships.

How does one go about taking swift action? Here are some suggestions. First and foremost, it's important that your alienated child or children start seeing an experienced PA/PAS mental health professional for an assessment, possible diagnosis, and treatment as soon as possible. A lot of parents don't recognize that their children may be depressed, experiencing trauma, or other difficulties in their lives. Taking your child or children to a clinician is not about judging, blaming, or shaming a parent. It's also not about making your child feel like he/she is at fault. Rather, it's about understanding and investigating your child's situation to bring about healing. An experienced PA/PAS therapist will provide age and developmentally appropriate therapeutic interventions such as play therapy; art therapy; trauma therapy; creative metaphors; videos/computer games specifically designed for helping alienated children; role-playing; cognitive-behavior therapy to help reduce stress, anxiety, fears, and alter mistaken perceptions about both parents; as well as a whole host of other supportive measures.

The therapy process may take some time before results are demonstrable. Don't expect to see any changes in your alienated child's behaviors within a few sessions. You and your ex-partner will need to be patient and not have unfair or unrealistic expectations for the child in question or the therapist. It's important to feel hopeful and optimistic that change can result from your child or children engaging in the counseling process. Please keep in mind, however, that even the most experienced, skilled, highly respected, and recommended therapists cannot help all alienated families. There is no magic potion, pill, or vaccination that can be given. Rather, a skilled therapist will devise an appropriate treatment plan after the assessment phase and provide the tools necessary to help the child and the rest of the family. Like other members of the family, the child ultimately is the one who has to make the choice to change his/her own behaviors. Similar to alienating parents, some alienated children refuse to see the truth because their delusional thinking has become so ingrained.

... The therapy process may take some time before results are demonstrable. Don't expect to see any changes in your alienated child's behaviors within a few sessions ...

Unless a court order states otherwise, both you and the alienating parent need to have a say in selecting an appropriate therapist for your child or children. Just as it's inappropriate and wrong for an alienating parent to take a child to a mental health professional without your knowledge and written informed consent when there's joint custody and/or joint guardianship in place, the same holds true if you were to do it behind the alienator's back.

It's best not to send your child or children to a therapist whom you and/or your ex-spouse have seen before. It's recommended that you choose someone new who has no history of your personal and family circumstances. Even though psychotherapists are taught to work with objective facts and not formulate preconceived notions about clients, sometimes the latter isn't so easy to do when a lengthy therapeutic relationship with various members of a family already exists.

A therapist experienced and skilled with PA/PAS cases will need to collaborate with you, your ex, and child plus take a neutral stance. Please don't expect the therapist to be on your side. An alienator and alienated child would quickly notice complete distrust, disparagement, and malignment by the therapist. They'd likely cease the therapy instantly.

...It's best not to send your child or children to a therapist whom you and/or your ex-spouse have seen before. It's recommended that you choose someone new who has no history of your personal and family circumstances ...

Be aware of any therapist who only wants to team up with the alienator and your child. If you're excluded for any reason, then you need to consult with your attorney immediately for intervention. It's just not possible for a professional to make an appropriate assessment without seeing all parties involved.

With that said, there are clinicians out there who will only choose to work with the alienated child and the alienator. In doing so, these clinicians run the risk of creating complete family annihilation. They get so caught up in the alienator and child's manipulation and delusional thinking that they lose sight of the realities of PAS. They may even form a strong bias against the target parent.

There are known cases where clinicians will write letters to judges outlining recommendations for supervised access—or even worse—

recommendations for a restraining order to be placed between the target parent and child. Other shocking instances involve clinicians reporting that target parents have serious psychiatric conditions even though the two have never met.

I've often asked myself with disbelief, "Why is it that some professionals are not able to see through the calculating, conniving, and underhanded ways of an alienator especially when he/she has never met the target parent and heard his/her side of the story? Why are these therapists not rescuing the child in question from the emotional abuse and trauma?" The only answer I've come up with so far is they just don't have any understanding of PA/PAS and the dynamics involved.

Coming to a mutual parental joint decision about whom your child or children should see is not an easy thing to do. In fact, the chances of getting both parents to agree to counseling for a child is remote partially because the alienating parent and programmed child don't want it. Generally, most alienators will do anything in their power to sabotage any efforts to rekindle the relationship between the child and alienated parent. The last thing they want is for a child to see an effective therapist who can help make this happen.

... Coming to a mutual parental joint decision about whom your child or children should see is not an easy thing to do ...

When you and your ex-partner are not able to come to a mutual decision, then you can each independently request recommendations from third-parties you both know, for example: teachers, friends, a family dentist, a family physician, a member of the clergy, or a past or present therapist. Then you and your ex can each write down half a dozen names of recommended therapists in your order of preference. The first therapist that appears on both lists is nominated the person for your children to see.

If that suggestion backfires for any reason, then you need to speak to an attorney right away. He or she can prepare and send a letter to you and the alienating parent providing the names of three recommended therapists for your children and the reasons for the recommendation. Hopefully, you and your ex-partner will be able to mutually agree on one of the three recommendations. If the alienating parent refuses to do so, then the attorney will likely send the alienating parent a second letter basically stating, "Please don't make me have to take you to court to set up a court-appointed parenting coordinator and/or therapist for the children in question". When the alienator resists the second letter from the attorney, legal decisions such as a court order are promptly set in motion to help offset the progression of alienation.

It's important for you to be aware that no specific label of PA or PAS needs to be provided to a court. Judges can make decisions from listening to narratives of the behavior of a child and the parents without requiring the terms parental alienation or parental alienation syndrome. Getting the right therapist appointed immediately by a court is critical even when a child is in the mild range of alienation. The legal process in and of itself can eat up a lot of time while the clock continues to tick and the child goes from mild to moderate to severe alienation.

...Getting the right therapist appointed immediately by a court is critical even when a child is in the mild range of alienation ...

Parenting coordinators can be very helpful with mild parental alienation cases. Whether both parents agree to seek the service of a parenting coordinator or one is court-referred, the parents learn how to communicate effectively and receive other supportive measures to help offset the progression of PAS.

I'm also of the opinion that experienced and skilled mental health professionals should see all members of a family even when the parental alienation is in the mild range. At this stage, the clinician can help strengthen the relationship between the alienated parent and the child and help reduce the enmeshment between the alienating parent and the child.

With moderate PAS cases, greater interventions are necessary.

In general, both parents need to seek the services of a parenting coordinator. All members of the alienated family also require more intensive therapeutic interventions. It's my opinion that a combination of individual and family counseling sessions are necessary with all parties.

In some cases, it's appropriate for multiple clinicians to be involved with the various members of an alienated family. If this is the case, it's important that all the therapists work in a collaborative process and share the same opinions on the nature of the difficulties in the alienated family. Multiple clinicians working with various members of an alienated family must also ensure they are working together in agreement with the treatment approaches being employed and toward the agreed upon therapeutic goals. If one or more clinicians do not see eye to eye on the nature, goals, and treatment approaches, then swift action needs to be taken with respect to finding ones who do.

... In some cases, it's appropriate for multiple clinicians to be involved with the various members of an alienated family ...

With severe PAS cases, finding the most effective therapeutic interventions for the alienated family becomes more complex. Some traditional therapies tend not to work well with severely alienated children and youths because their irrational and delusional beliefs have become so entrenched and difficult to quash. Through the years, mental health professionals have not consistently agreed upon what's the most effective treatment approach for severe cases.

Some have argued that it's best for the child to be removed from the alienating parent and transferred to the care of the targeted parent (Gardner, 2001) while others argue that the child should remain with the alienator and undergo various forms of psychotherapeutic treatment (Sullivan & Kelly, 2001).

Recently, Dr. Douglas Darnall (2010) implemented an innovative treatment approach called "Reunification Therapy (RT)", which requires the entire family's involvement. His book called *Beyond*

Divorce Casualties: Reunifying the Alienated Family (2010) extensively details the treatment protocols, some of which include the following:

First and foremost, a court order is absolutely necessary to stipulate the names of all members of the alienated family who must participate in the RT. This is done to help ensure program compliance and outcome success amongst all family members involved. A RT mental health professional is assigned by the court, and the professional must not have had any prior relationship with any family members. The court defines the ground rules, the roles of all family members involved, as well as the role of the therapist. The therapist is responsible for monitoring and reporting information to the court including non-compliance issues. Therefore, the court is also considered the client and there is no protection of confidentiality between the parties involved (the judge, the therapist(s), the parents, the children, and any other court-appointed personnel). There's only one exception regarding the rule of no confidentiality amongst all parties; any past mental health or medical records of the parents remain confidential and must not be disclosed. Insurance companies do not fully or even partially reimburse the cost of RT and the court order defines who will be responsible to pay for RT. Darnall's RT is grounded by family systems theory, cognitive-behavior theory, and attachment theory, however, no outcome studies have been conducted on his treatment approach to date (public presentation, May 28, 2011).

Additionally, Dr. Richard A. Warshak has developed a leading-edge educational and experiential treatment program called *Family Bridges: A Workshop for Troubled and Alienated Parent-Child Relationships* (Warshak, 2010a, 2010b; Warshak & Otis, 2010). This intensive treatment program is based on Dr. Randy Rand's prototype that was developed in the early 1990s to help recovered children who had been abducted establish a healthy reintegration back into family life. Approximately six years ago, Dr. Randy Rand and Dr. Deirdre

...First and foremost, a court order is absolutely necessary to stipulate the names of all members of the alienated family who must participate in the RT ...

Rand began to mentor Dr. Warshak on the program. Together, they cultivated and fine-tuned *Family Bridges* specifically for severely alienated and estranged children and their rejected parents. To date, other professionals have received *Family Bridges* training to be able to help reunify rejected parents and severely alienated children and youth in various parts of the United States and Canada.

Darnall and Warshak's novel therapeutic approaches hold some promising results. If you believe that your child or youth has reached a severe level of PAS—and for whatever reasons swift action wasn't taken to get therapy—or your son or daughter experienced one or more failed therapy attempts, please don't despair. There is hope. In light of the fact that courts are now dealing with varying degrees of PAS cases, it's apparent that some judges are making positive rulings especially when extreme cases are present. Here are a couple of examples.

> ... To date, other professionals have received Family Bridges training to be able to help reunify rejected parents and severely alienated children and youth in various parts of the United States and Canada...

In *Doerman v. Doerman, 2002 Ohio App. LEXIS 3183* (Ohio Ct. App. June 24, 2002), an Ohio Court of Appeal granted custody to an alienated father after receiving substantial psychological evidence that the children in question were experiencing severe PAS. The alienating mother prolonged efforts to end the custody dispute, coached the children to report certain things over the phone, refused to cooperate during the father's visiting times, made false allegations of abuse by the targeted parent, and ignored court orders.

In May 2008, Makin, a news reporter with The *Globe and Mail*, reported a landmark PAS case in Toronto that revealed how a male adolescent was systematically programmed by his father to hate his mother, and likely women in general. The alienating parent had a long history of engaging in outlandish behaviors, forcing his son to follow suit, and refusing to cooperate by not allowing the mother to have access to their son. The Ontario Supreme Court judge accepted that severe PAS was occurring. He ordered the teenager to attend

Dr. Warshak's program in Texas since there were no appropriate Canadian resources available for this severely alienated youth. The young male was flown to the U.S. facility against his will and his mother was flown to the program separately. They were reunited and underwent intensive interventions to help deprogram the son. The young teen also received aftercare from an Ontario psychologist upon returning home.

In March 2009, *The Winnipeg Free Press* published another interesting PAS case whereby an alienating mother was banned by a Supreme Court judge in British Columbia from seeing her adolescent daughter for over a year. The maternal grandmother was also banned from having any contact with the youth for over a year. Although it's rare for Canadian judges to make rulings that entail banning an alienator from having any contact with a child or youth for a specific period of time, in this particular court case it was found that the mother alleged extreme emotional abuse by the targeted parent without any objective evidence. The mother was also court ordered to pay a significant amount of money for her daughter to receive psychotherapy in addition to the child support she was already contributing. Typically speaking, Canadian courts tend to strike a balance in access between parents in family alienation cases. In this case, the judge believed it was not in the best interests of the youth.

...Typically speaking, Canadian courts tend to strike a balance in access between parents in family alienation cases. In this case, the judge believed it was not in the best interests of the youth ...

In the event that you are having difficulty finding an experienced PA/PAS therapist or are feeling unsatisfied with the therapist you're working with, please don't hesitate to contact me via email at drkathleenreay@gmail.com. I'll do my best to help you with your difficulties. ❧

Time for Self-Reflection

In your case, have you found that the seeds of PAS have sprouted quickly? If so, in what ways? Please describe in detail.

_____

_____

_____

_____

_____

_____

_____

_____

_____

_____

_____

_____

_____

_____

_____

Do you agree that it's necessary for an alienated parent to take swift action to help stop the progression of PAS? Please explain.

_____

_____

_____

_____

_____

_____

_____

_____

What have you chosen to do so far with respect to the aforementioned question?

_____

_____

_____

_____

_____

How do you feel about the decision you've made so far?

_____

_____

_____

_____

_____

_____

_____

What has been the overall outcome since taking steps so far? Has it been a positive or negative experience for you?

_____

_____

_____

_____

_____

_____

_____

_____

Is there any need to do something else at this point in time? If so, what do you plan to do? How do you plan to accomplish this?

_____

_____

_____

_____

_____

_____

_____

_____

What were the most significant things you learned from reading this chapter?

_____

_____

_____

_____

_____

_____

_____

_____

Additional Comments:

_____

_____

_____

_____

_____

Chapter Nineteen
Choosing a Mental Health Professional

When you begin considering the need for mental health support, it's suggested that you first decide on what your needs are. With respect to PA or PAS, there is a wide array of mental health services offered as well as a wide array of professionals who specifically offer them.

254 Toxic Divorce: A Workbook for Alienated Parents

When you begin considering the need for mental health support, it's suggested that you first decide on what your needs are. With respect to PA or PAS, there is a wide array of mental health services offered as well as a wide array of professionals who specifically offer them.

What are your specific needs?

... With respect to PA or PAS, there is a wide array of mental health services offered as well as a wide array of professionals who specifically offer them ...

Examples:

❏ I need individual counseling.

❏ I need family counseling.

❏ I need a counselor to help my alienated child or children.

❏ I need a Child Custody Evaluator.

❏ I need a Family Mediator.

❏ I need a Parenting Coordinator.

❏ I need two or more of the above-noted services.

Sometimes alienated parents start off with seeking individual counseling services for themselves. In other cases, targeted parents simultaneously or separately need more than one type of mental health service. Let's look at your situation. What are your present needs, if any? In your case, for instance, do you feel the need for individual counseling to help deal with the ramifications of being a targeted parent? Are you also feeling concerned about your alienated children's needs for therapy? If you answered yes to both questions, then it sounds like you desire a combination of individual counseling for yourself and perhaps individual/family counseling for your child/ children. The family counseling may include you, your ex, and your children.

It's also possible that you may need to seek the services of an experienced child custody evaluator as well as counseling. If this is the case, you will need to seek the services of at least two different mental health professionals. Ethical codes of conduct in the mental health profession state that it is not appropriate for a professional in the field to have a dual relationship with clients. An example of a dual relationship in PA or PAS situations would be to provide therapy and conduct a child custody evaluation for the same family.

Please keep in mind that alienation is very difficult to reverse after it reaches a certain point. As such, the children can be permanently damaged plus the relationship between the child and the alienated parent will be much harder to recover.

To help you make an informed decision about your needs, it's important to understand the differences between a psychiatrist, psychologist, counselor, social worker, child custody evaluator, family mediator, and parenting coordinator. Here they are:

... Ethical codes of conduct in the mental health profession state that it is not appropriate for a professional in the field to have a dual relationship with clients ...

Psychiatrists

Psychiatrists are specialists in the field of medicine. In terms of training, before entering into the specialty of psychiatry, an individual must first graduate from medical school as a doctor (MD). Generally speaking, most psychiatrists are trained to view medical problems from a biological approach. Thus, mental health problems including depression and anxiety are perceived as biochemical imbalances. Some psychiatrists also conduct research studies on the effectiveness of drugs. Typically, psychiatrists treat patients with prescribed medication and do not offer psychotherapy. Seeing a psychiatrist is similar to seeing a general or family physician. In most cases, little time is spent with them during each appointment. Keep in mind that a well-qualified psychiatrist can diagnose PA or PAS and testify in court as an expert witness.

Psychologists

Like psychiatrists, psychologists must take rigorous training. Psychologists, however, do not go to medical school. Rather, they typically are required to graduate with a bachelor's degree in psychology or a related social science, a master's degree in counseling or clinical psychology, and a doctorate degree (Ph.D. or Psy.D.) in clinical psychology. Some licensed psychologists who work with PA and PAS cases may have a doctorate degree in forensic psychology instead of clinical psychology. In many countries, completion of a doctorate degree in counseling, clinical, or forensic psychology is required prior to being allowed to register as a psychologist. Instead of viewing mental health problems as biochemical in nature, psychologists utilize a more holistic approach. Psychologists place greater emphasis on understanding an individual's background, personality features, sociocultural background, and so on. Sessions are based on a personalized approach that suits the needs of the client. Treatment goals and treatment plans are mutually agreed upon by the psychologist and client. Each session is generally one hour in length. Traditionally, psychologists do not have the ability to prescribe medications but this is slowly changing. Already, in some U.S. States psychologists have licensing privileges to prescribe medication besides offering psychotherapy. Some psychologists also conduct research studies on various areas of interest in the field of psychology. Similar to psychiatrists, well qualified licensed or registered psychologists can also diagnose PA or PAS and testify in court as expert witnesses.

... Typically, psychiatrists treat patients with prescribed medication and do not offer psychotherapy. Seeing a psychiatrist is similar to seeing a general or family physician ...

Counselors

The term counselor is considered loosey-goosey because some individuals practice informally and call themselves counselors. However, in some instances they may not have graduated from high school nor have gone to college or university to earn a diploma or degree. There are certain public safety precautions you need to be aware of. To practice formally as a licensed or registered counselor, an individual generally has to complete a minimum of a bachelor's degree in psychology plus earn a master's degree in counseling, marriage and family, or clinical psychology, which includes undertaking supervised clinical supervision and/or residency requirements. Similar to psychologists, most counselors utilize a holistic, eclectic approach to working with individuals, couples and families. Counselors are typically not trained to provide diagnostic testing and assessment procedures like psychologists do. Each session with a registered or licensed counselor is generally one hour in length.

... Similar to psychologists, most counselors utilize a holistic, eclectic approach to working with individuals, couples and families ...

Social Workers

Social workers typically have a minimum of a bachelor's degree in social work. In most work settings, a master's degree in social work is required. Many social workers support disadvantaged individuals who need assistance with managing certain tasks in life. Social workers may work in social service settings, hospital settings, mental health settings, correctional settings, schools, child welfare settings, physical rehabilitation settings, and in community development. Some social workers advocate for social justice policy at differing levels of government and/or conduct research studies. A registered or licensed social worker is trained in psychotherapy and helps persons of all ages deal with a variety of mental health and daily living difficulties to improve their overall functioning.

Child Custody Evaluators

Child custody evaluators are qualified and experienced mental health professionals who act as impartial examiners. It is a highly specialized area that requires extensive training, supervision, and up-to-date knowledge with respect to various psycho-legal issues and standards that are set forth in the jurisdiction in which the evaluation is requested. In the vast majority of cases, the evaluator will be a licensed psychologist (clinical or forensic) or a psychiatrist who also has taken post-graduate specialized training. In some regions, evaluators may have a master's degree in counseling, social work, or clinical psychology plus have taken specialized training. Child custody evaluators generally work for family court systems or carry out their roles and responsibilities privately. In terms of their ethical code of conduct, child custody evaluators strive to be accurate, fair, objective, and independent in their assessments and are encouraged to use peer reviewed research to back up certain claims in their assessment reports.

... In the vast majority of cases, the evaluator will be a licensed psychologist (clinical or forensic) or a psychiatrist who also has taken post-graduate specialized training ...

Family Mediators

Certified Family Relations Mediators, Certified Family Financial Mediators, and Certified Comprehensive Family Mediators have taken appropriate coursework and have received their respective designations through an approved college, university and/or national association. Quite commonly, mediators are social workers, lawyers, psychologists, or other professionals. Their roles and responsibilities include providing education and offering effective alternatives to resolving conflicts and reaching agreements on the division of property and other assets, support payments, child custody and access issues, and other family-related matters. Similar to counselors, it is important that you choose a family mediator who is registered in your area and subscribes to an ethical code of professional conduct. Additionally, you are encouraged to speak to a lawyer or attorney first before seeking the services of a mediator.

Mediators are not permitted to offer legal advice. Also, family mediation is not appropriate for everyone, especially in situations where violence or abuse has taken place. One of the major benefits of seeking family mediation is that it is relatively inexpensive and less time consuming than going through legal and court systems.

Parenting Coordinators

Parenting coordinators are experienced counselors, social workers, psychologists, and lawyers/attorneys who have taken specialized training in mediating and arbitrating parenting disputes. The primary focus is on helping separated parents recognize what is in the best interests of their children. The parenting coordinator acts as a neutral decision-maker who can help resolve various types of parenting conflicts as they arise. A primary goal is to help minimize further conflict and to help offset the need to use the court system. Some courts will mandate parents to seek help through a parenting coordinator. In other cases, parents can hire a parenting coordinator on their own initiative. Parenting coordination is a relatively new profession. At the present time, parenting coordinators are not legalized to work in all U.S. states and Canadian provinces. To date, California, Oregon, Washington, Arizona, Texas, Florida, Colorado, New Mexico, Hawaii, Georgia, Massachusetts, Oklahoma, North Carolina, Ohio, Vermont, and Idaho have parenting coordination services available. In Canada, parenting coordinators are currently found in British Columbia, Alberta, Manitoba, and Ontario. Similar to family mediation, parenting coordination is not appropriate for everyone. Generally speaking, this type of professional help works best for parents who already have some type of permanent arrangement in place about parenting issues. This type of professional service is not meant to resolve child custody, guardianship, and access issues. However, once the latter problems are solved, whether by a court order or through a written agreement, parenting coordinators can be of great service. Similar to family mediation, parenting coordination

... The parenting coordinator acts as a neutral decision-maker who can help resolve various types of parenting conflicts as they arise ...

services is relatively inexpensive and less time consuming than the court system.

Tips for Interviewing Mental Health Professionals

After you have decided on whether you need a psychiatrist, psychologist, counselor, social worker, child custody evaluator, family mediator, and/or parenting coordinator, the next suggested step is to prepare for interviewing them. I cannot stress enough how important it is for you to interview a mental health professional if you plan on retaining one privately. Just as not all vehicle door handles are the same, not all mental health professionals in their chosen discipline are either!

It's a good idea to ask as many friends or acquaintances you meet through in-person or online PAS support groups who they would recommend. If you're open to it, discuss with them what your specific needs are. Then ask, "Have you seen this person yourself?" Or, "How did you hear about this particular mental health professional?" "Have you heard about any other psychologists (or some other type of mental health professional) in the area who may be as good just in case this one is not available to work with me?"

... interview a mental health professional if you plan on retaining one privately. Just as not all vehicle door handles are the same, not all mental health professionals in their chosen discipline are either! ...

Next phone or email the mental health professional. Please keep in mind that it's possible that you may not be able to speak to him or her directly. Some mental health professionals have office assistants who look after scheduling appointments and other frontline duties. In these cases, some professionals choose not to engage in interviews over the phone. Still some choose not to have office assistants and look after scheduling appointments over the phone or via email themselves. Do not feel put off or surprised if a professional that you would like to interview is not able to talk over the telephone and it's necessary to schedule an initial consultation to meet him/her.

Never be afraid to ask important questions either over the phone or during the initial consultation. You are in charge here. You are in the hiring process and therefore it's important to determine whether the professional is the right fit for you and/or your family.

Always prepare basic information for the interview such as what is suggested in the sample interview form in this chapter. Another thing that I can't stress enough is to ensure that the mental health professional that you choose to hire is experienced, trained, and familiar with PA and PAS. There are numerous mental health professionals who don't have a clue about PA or PAS. In other cases, "many mental health professionals have heard of the term PAS but confuse it with 'parental alienation' and simply do not understand the symptoms, criteria, and scope of PAS as a form of child abuse" (Gardner, 2002d, p. 101).

Additionally, therapist alienation can occur when a mental health professional is not experienced nor has the proper knowledge and skill-set to work with alienated families (Garber, 2004). Quite frankly, some professionals like attorneys or lawyers can be taken advantage of by alienating parents who intend to hold their children hostage from the other parent. Alienated parents need to be aware that there are also certain organizations and other support systems in both the United States and Canada that do not support or maintain children's rights to have relationships with both parents. Rather, they support a parent's ability to alienate a child from the other parent.

... Always prepare basic information for the interview such as what is suggested in the sample interview form in this chapter ...

Therapist alienation occurs when a party outside of the therapeutic alliance, particularly a significant other, exposes the patient to negatives about the therapy or the therapist. The result is contamination of the ... [doctor-patient or counselor-patient relationship] causing the patient to feel less secure in the therapeutic relationship, impeding therapeutic progress and presumably decreasing the therapist's threat to the family's existing dynamic balance. Therapist alienation is manifest as otherwise inexplicable resistance, impasse, or in the extreme, rupture of the therapeutic alliance (Garber, 2004, p. 358).

Additionally, children and youth need to know about laws in place which protect their rights to have relationships with both parents; information about legal capacity of children's decision-making, which is typically ignored in family court; and child welfare proceedings.

Thus, when you are making an informed decision about choosing the right mental health professional for individual and family counseling purposes, ask for clarification on what role he/she will play in working with you. Garber (2004, p. 359) adds, "Just as the adult conflict can lead the child to feel pulled toward each caregiver and away from the other, his or her trust in and cooperation with the therapist can come to be experienced as an act of loyalty to one caregiver or betrayal of another." All in all, don't waste your time or that of the mental health professional if he/she is not experienced in working with PA or PAS cases.

... when you are making an informed decision about choosing the right mental health professional for individual and family counseling purposes, ask for clarification on what role he/she will play in working with you...

Also, don't waste your time or that of the mental health professional if he/she is not licensed or registered to practice in your state or province. Experience and licensing are two different things and are not synonymous. Quite frankly, when scouting out the right professional for you and/or your family ask right away if he/she is licensed or registered to practice. If the answer is no, then thank the person for their time and hang up. Although having a state or provincial license to practice is no indicator of competence, it's an essential requirement you need to screen for. By choosing a licensed mental health professional you will have legal recourse in the rare event that you receive grossly incompetent or inappropriate service delivery.

It's also a good idea to verify the current licensing or registration status with the state licensing body or the provincial regulatory body that they claimed to have. Simply go to the website for the professional regulatory body and click on "Verify Registration Status" or "List of Professional Members" to determine if the information given is accurate. Most, if not all, regulatory bodies will be able to tell you if the professional has any past or current complaints against him/her. In the event that this kind of information is not listed on the regulatory body's website, a quick call should provide the information.

Lastly, when an initial appointment has been scheduled, ask, "What information would you like me to bring or have for our first consultation? Is there a way for me to prepare for this meeting to make the most of it?" I've never met a mental health professional who was not impressed hearing those kinds of questions from a prospective new patient. ✍

... It's also a good idea to verify the current licensing or registration status with the state licensing body or the provincial regulatory body that they claimed to have ...

Here is Casey's Sample Interview Form for you to peruse. Additionally, you can use the blank interview form contained at the end of this chapter for your own use.

Casey's Sample Interview Form to Select an Appropriate Mental Health Professional

What's my purpose for hiring a mental health professional? Be specific.

I'm feeling stressed, depressed and angry. I feel I need individual counseling.

Professional's Name: ___Dr. A. Nelson___

Professional's Credentials: ___Ph.D., Clinical Psychology___

Professional's Education: ___BA – majored in psychology – University of Washington. MS–Clinical Psychology and Ph.D. Clinical Psychology at University of Oregon in 1989.___

Professional's post-graduate training: ___Child Psychology, child custody & divorce issues, parenting skills, divorce mediation, advanced cognitive–behavior therapy plus training in many other areas in psychology.___

Is he or she licensed or registered?

☒ Yes. Who is she/he licensed or registered with?

Washington State Psychological Association.

❏ No. Feel free to ask why he/she is not licensed to practice, or move on to the next mental health professional on your list.

Ask the mental health professional if he/she has ever heard of PAS. If the professional has no knowledge of it, do not proceed with this candidate. Don't waste your time or the professional's time. Move on to someone else on your interview list. If aware of PAS, ask the professional to describe his/her understanding of it to you, and if he/she believes in PAS? Don't hesitate to ask as many questions as you want.

☒ Yes, the professional is aware of PAS and believes in PAS. Ask her/him to elaborate.

He described the differences between PA and PAS. He believes PAS is a valid syndrome. He mentioned there are different levels of PAS — mild, moderate and severe and each type requires specific treatment methods. He said he enjoys the challenge of working with alienated families.

_____
_____
_____
_____

❏   No, the professional is not aware of PAS. Move on to someone else on your interview list.

Professional's past and present experience working with PAS cases: _____
He estimates that he has worked with at least 50 different PAS cases. He's mainly worked with alienated parents and their children either individually or in family counseling because the alienating parents refused to attend. He's also worked with a lot of court-ordered cases. The alienators were forced to attend, too. He's been an expert witness in court at least 27 times.
_____
_____

Ask the professional how he/she will likely be able to help you out with your needs:
Dr. Nelson says he would like to learn more about my family situation. He plans to give me some questionnaires to fill out and talk to me. Then he will come up with a treatment plan to help me deal with my stress, anger and depression. He likes to provide cognitive-behavior therapy and other approaches.
_____
_____
_____
_____
_____

Cost of appointments:

$150.00 per 1 hour session.

Does the professional accept any health care insurance coverage, if applicable?

Yes

Is the professional covered by my Employee and Family Assistance Program, if applicable?

Yes

Ask the professional to use a scale ranging from 0 – 10 on how willing and committed he or she is to help you and/or your family right away (0 = not at all and 10 = completely willing and committed to helping you and/or your family right away):

10/10

Verification with the State Licensing Board or Provincial Regulatory Board:

☒ Yes   ☒   Via the Professional Regulatory Body's Website

                ❏   Via telephone

                ☒   The professional is in good standing

                ❏   The professional is not in good standing

❏ No

Your overall impression:

He's the most impressive person I've interviewed. He seemed very interested in me. He was nice and had a good sense of humor. He was easy to talk to. He listened well. Dr. Nelson has a good understanding of PAS. Lots of experience too.

My Interview Form to Select an Appropriate Mental Health Professional

What's my purpose for hiring a mental health professional? Be specific.

_____

_____

_____

_____

_____

_____

_____

_____

_____

_____

_____

_____

Professional's Name: _____

Professional's Credentials: _____

_____

_____

_____

Professional's Education: _____

Professional's post-graduate training: _____

_____

_____

_____

_____

Is he or she licensed or registered?

❏   Yes. Who is she/he licensed or registered with?

_____

❏   No. Feel free to ask why he/she is not licensed to practice, or move on to the next mental health professional on your list.

_____

Ask the mental health professional if he/she has ever heard of PAS. If the professional has no knowledge of it, do not proceed with this candidate. Don't waste your time or the professional's time. Move on to someone else on your interview list. If aware of PAS, ask the professional to describe his/her understanding of it to you, and if he/she believes in PAS? Don't hesitate to ask as many questions as you want.

❏ Yes, the professional is aware of PAS and believes in PAS. Ask her/him to elaborate.

_____
_____
_____
_____
_____
_____
_____
_____
_____
_____
_____

_____
_____
_____
_____

❏   No, the professional is not aware of PAS. Move on to someone else on your interview list.

Professional's past and present experience working with PAS cases: _____
_____
_____
_____
_____
_____
_____
_____
_____

Ask the professional how he/she will likely be able to help you out with your needs:
_____
_____
_____
_____
_____
_____
_____
_____
_____
_____
_____

Cost of appointments:

_____

Does the professional accept any health care insurance coverage, if applicable?

_____

Is the professional covered by my Employee and Family Assistance Program, if applicable?

_____

Ask the professional to use a scale ranging from 0 – 10 on how willing and committed he or she is to help you and/or your family right away (0 = not at all and 10 = completely willing and committed to helping you and/or your family right away):

_____

Verification with the State Licensing Board or Provincial Regulatory Board:

❑ Yes   ❑   Via the Professional Regulatory Body's Website

               ❑   Via telephone

               ❑   The professional is in good standing

               ❑   The professional is not in good standing

❑ No

Your overall impression:

_____

_____

_____

_____

_____

_____

_____

_____

_____

_____

_____

_____

_____

_____

_____

_____

_____

_____

_____

_____

_____

_____

_____

_____

_____

_____

_____

Chapter Twenty
Choosing an Attorney

Similar to choosing an appropriate mental health professional for your PA or PAS case, it's vital to obtain the professional services of a highly experienced, well-qualified family law attorney who is familiar with both.

Similar to choosing an appropriate mental health professional for your PA or PAS case, it's vital to obtain the professional services of a highly experienced, well-qualified family law attorney who is familiar with both. PA and PAS cases can be exceedingly complicated issues to handle in separation/divorce and child custody matters. In fact, circumstances concerning PA and PAS can be at times thorny to prove in a court of law and can also be onerous and time-consuming. If you're being unjustifiably alienated from your child or children following a separation or divorce, it's crucial for you to seek the services of a well-qualified family law attorney as soon as possible. A qualified and experienced professional will have the ability to not only ascertain your legal rights and options, but he/she will also be able to work in your and your child's best interests. Remember, the outcome of a family law case is central to your life and your future as well as your children's lives and futures. Taking the time and making the effort to select the right legal expert at the outset can often save you time, energy, stress, and money in the long run.

... If you're being unjustifiably alienated from your child or children following a separation or divorce, it's crucial for you to seek the services of a well-qualified family law attorney as soon as possible ...

The greater the level of severity in a PAS case, the greater the need to obtain a legal expert who has the knowledge and skill-set to engage in swift action against the alienator.

Prior to providing you some tips for choosing an appropriate legal expert, let me provide a word of caution here. You may recall in chapter 19 that therapist alienation is something that can occur and is important to watch out for. Unfortunately, but true, some attorneys and even judges can get caught up in third-party alienation. The law is black and white. Given the adversarial nature of representing one party against the other in separation, divorce, and child custody proceedings—plus factoring in various delays caused by court proceedings—attorneys and judges can contribute to the level of severity of PAS (Johnston & Campbell, 1988; Lund, 1992). As one psychologist points out, "If contact is stopped between parent and child, a pattern is likely to develop such that it will be difficult to mend the relationship. Delays inherent in formal court proceedings make it difficult to use orders to reinstate contact" (Lund, 1992, paragraph 3).

Tips for Choosing an Appropriate Legal Expert

Just as important as it is to interview a mental health professional for your needs, it's essential to interview legal experts. I recommend that you take the time to meet with several attorneys before selecting the one that seems like the best fit for your situation.

Word-of-Mouth

Although there are many ways to choose the right attorney, word-of-mouth is one of the best, most reliable ways to go about it. Ask friends, acquaintances, co-workers, and family members if they know of or have used a good family law attorney.

Contact the Local Bar Association

The local Bar Association will also be able to provide you with names of family law experts in your area who are experienced with PA and PAS cases.

Ask a Non-Family Law Attorney

Perhaps you know an attorney who practices in another area of law. If so, ask him/her for a referral to a family law attorney who is experienced with PA or PAS cases.

...Just as important as it is to interview a mental health professional for your needs, it's essential to interview legal experts ...

PA and PAS Experience

Given attorneys specialize in a vast array of legal matters, ensure that your attorney practices exclusively and has experience in family law matters, especially with PA and PAS cases. Don't waste your time or the attorney's if it turns out he/she has no experience with PA or PAS cases.

Find Out the Number of PA & PAS Cases Won or Lost

Generally, the easiest way to determine how many cases an attorney has won or lost with respect to PA and PAS is to simply ask. You can also find this kind of information by searching online or contact the state or provincial court system. Many family law attorneys tend to practice in the same jurisdiction or courthouse. It's possible in some instances to be able to contact the state judicial offices or check their websites online. The availability of the latter types of searches do vary widely throughout the US and Canada.

Integrity

Determine whether or not the attorney that you interview seems honest and ethical. It may seem tempting to hire one who has a reputation for acting like a pit bull in court, but if an attorney is willing to be unethical in some circumstances, then you need to ask yourself why you should feel confident that he/she is actually dealing honestly with you.

Reputation

Prior to hiring an attorney ensure that he/she is a member in good standing of the local bar association. Don't be afraid to ask the prospective attorney if a report or claim has been made against him/her. It's a good idea to check with your local bar association to ensure the attorney you're considering hiring has not had any malpractice claims against him/her. Additionally, ask around your community. Find out from others if he/she is known for being

... Given attorneys specialize in a vast array of legal matters, ensure that your attorney practices exclusively and has experience in family law matters, especially with PA and PAS cases ...

ethical, competent, trustworthy, reliable, and meticulous in working with PA or PAS cases.

Personality and Communication Styles

Make sure that the attorney you plan to hire really clicks with your own personality and communication styles. The two of you will be spending a considerable amount of time working together. Even though an attorney may sound great from word-of-mouth references or even on paper, it doesn't necessarily mean the two of you will click. Being able to communicate effectively is vital. A really good legal expert will be able to clearly communicate details of your case and tell you what he/she plans to do and why. You don't want to end up feeling stymied, frustrated, and angry with your attorney if communication is not happening. Be choosy!

Availability

Availability is certainly going to be a big factor in your decision-making process. During the interview process, explore how you will be able to discuss issues with each attorney. Some legal experts work alone and may not be available at times while some have paralegals and other legal assistants on the frontlines. Prior to hiring an attorney, ensure there's someone available in the office to answer questions and to schedule appointments in a timely manner.

... Make sure that the attorney you plan to hire really clicks with your own personality and communication styles. The two of you will be spending a considerable amount of time working together ...

Fees

Similar to hiring a mental health professional, you typically do get what you pay for. If your budget allows, it's best not to base your decision on fees only. Experience, the number of winning outcomes, integrity, reputation, communication style, personality style, and availability should all be important factors in the decision-making process. During your interview, clarify with the attorney the retainer required, if any, what the hourly rate is, what types of activities are billed, and how often you will be billed. ∞

Sally's Sample Interview Form is next for you to peruse. Additionally, you can use the blank interview form at the end of this chapter for your own use.

Sally's Interview Form to Select an Appropriate Legal Expert

What's my purpose for hiring an attorney? Be specific.

My husband is making this a long drawn out divorce battle. I believe he's alienating our children against me. It seems very real. I haven't seen or heard from the kids for nearly five weeks. I can't do this on my own and need a good attorney.

Attorney's Name: Albertine J. Gomez

Professional's Education: Loma Linda University, California – undergrad degree. University of Pennsylvania Law School, Family Law.

Professional's Credentials: J.D. (means Juris Doctor)

Recommended by: My friend Ana.

Is he or she licensed by the state or provincial bar association in the region you live in?

☑ Yes. Who is he/she licensed with? Admitted to State Bar of California in 1980.

☑ Yes. Is he/she a member in good standing with the bar association?

❏ No. If he/she answers no to the above, then move on to the next legal professional on your list to interview.

Ask the legal professional if he/she is experienced in working with PA or PAS cases. If not, move on to someone else on your interview list.

If the professional is experienced, then ask him/her to describe his/her understanding of it to you. Also, ask the professional if he/she believes in PAS and if so to elaborate? Ask as many questions as you want.

She has an abundant amount of experience. Said that PA is a general term and is often cited. PAS is the systematic denigration by one parent with the intent of alienating the child against the other parent. She believes in both PA and PAS. Told her all about my circumstances, including the fact that my husband supports no resolution and is dragging everything out. She said these types of divorce and child custody battles have become increasingly common since beginning her law practice. Ms. Gomez agrees there's too much animosity occurring and it must be heartbreaking. She agrees there's a need/urgency to get help for my children. Ms. Gomez said that it's sometimes difficult to get help without a judge ordering it. She's a family law specialist and doesn't practice in any other area.

❏ No, the professional is not aware of PAS. Move on to someone else on your interview list.

Professional's experience working with past and present PAS cases:

She's had an abundant amount of experience working with PA/PAS cases. While talking over the phone, she emailed one of the most recent PAS cases she won. She plans to send more information via email for me to review later. References will also be provided.

Ask how many cases he/she has won or lost? She didn't know the exact numbers but states she's definitely won more than lost. She provided info on how I can view the cases online to give me a good level of comfort.

Ask the professional how he/she will likely be able to help you out with your needs: Ms. Gomez says there's no such thing as a typical divorce or child custody case. Having learned a little bit about my circumstances, she says my case needs to be taken very seriously. She can act on it quickly and go before a judge on my behalf. She says that clear, specific, detailed and enforceable court orders often need to be made by judges so alienating parents will comply.

Clarify his/her fee structure. For example, what is his/her hourly rate? Will a retainer be required, if so, how much? What types of activities will be billed? How often will he/she bill you? Is there a payment plan option, etc.?

Her secretary will email me a document regarding what she charges in the way of fees and expenses up front before the representation begins. $262 per hour—attorney. Extra fees for paralegal and secretarial services. Initial retainer fee is $3,000. Everything will be in a written contract. I will also get periodic itemized billing which will list all charges so that I can review them and compare them to my written fee contract.

In terms of his/her availability, explore how you will potentially be able to discuss issues whenever you need to: We'll be able to discuss things by phone, email or in person when she's available. I can discuss anything with her secretary at any time.

Ask the professional to use a scale ranging from 0 – 10 on how willing and committed he/she is to help you and/or your family right away (0 = not at all and 10 = completely willing and committed to helping you and/or your family right away): 10

Verification with the State or Provincial Bar Association:

☑ Yes   ☑   Via the Bar Association's Website

❑   Via telephone

☑   The professional is in good standing

❑   The professional is not in good standing

❑ No

Your overall impression:

She sounds very capable, reliable, insightful and experienced. She sounded honest and trustworthy. I like her personality. She was easy to talk to. My friend says she's capable, reliable and reputable. Ana's case was won and the circumstances are similar. She's highly motivated and willing to get started right away. I'll review everything Ms. Gomez and her secretary send me. I'll also look up the online cases she told me about before making a final decision.

My Interview Form to Select an Appropriate Legal Expert

What's my purpose for hiring an attorney? Be specific.

_____

_____

_____

_____

_____

_____

Attorney's Name: _____

Professional's Education: _____

Professional's Credentials: _____

Recommended by: _____

Is he or she licensed by the state or provincial bar association in the region you live in?

❏   Yes. Who is he/she licensed with?_____

❏   Yes. Is he/she a member in good standing with the bar association?

❏   No.   If he/she answers no to the above, then move on to the next legal professional on your list to interview.

Ask the legal professional if he/she is experienced in working with PA or PAS cases. If not, move on to someone else on your interview list.

If the professional is experienced, then ask him/her to describe his/her understanding of it to you. Also, ask the professional if he/she believes in PAS and if so to elaborate? Ask as many questions as you want.

_____

_____

_____

_____

_____

_____

_____

_____

_____

_____

_____

_____

_____

_____

_____

_____

_____

_____

❑   No, the professional is not aware of PAS. Move on to someone else on your interview list.

Professional's experience working with past and present PAS cases: _____

_____

_____

_____

_____

_____

_____

_____

Ask how many cases he/she has won or lost? _____

_____

_____

_____

Ask the professional how he/she will likely be able to help you out with your needs:

_____

_____

_____

_____

_____

Clarify his/her fee structure. For example, what is his/her hourly rate? Will a retainer be required, if so, how much? What types of activities will be billed? How often will he/she bill you? Is there a payment plan option, etc.?

_____

_____

_____

_____

_____

_____

_____

In terms of his/her availability, explore how you will potentially be able to discuss issues whenever you need to: _____

_____

_____

_____

Ask the professional to use a scale ranging from 0 – 10 on how willing and committed he/she is to help you and/or your family right away (0 = not at all and 10 = completely willing and committed to helping you and/or your family right away): _____

Verification with the State or Provincial Bar Association:

❑ Yes   ❑ Via the Bar Association's Website

       ❑ Via telephone

       ❑ The professional is in good standing

       ❑ The professional is not in good standing

❑ No

Your overall impression:

_____

_____

_____

_____

_____

_____

_____

Chapter Twenty-One
Never Give Up

*Even though your ex-partner may believe
that your children are better off not having
contact with you and your children have been
programmed to believe that, it's not true.
Whether you believe that or not, your children
need you in their lives.*

S ir Winston Churchill once said, "Never, never, never give up!" If you are an alienated parent, please don't despair or ever give up. Even though your ex-partner may believe that your children are better off not having contact with you and your children have been programmed to believe that, it's not true. Whether you believe that or not, your children need you in their lives.

...If you and your children are victims of PAS, an unjustifiable alienation, then you have every right to be in their lives ...

If you and your children are victims of PAS, an unjustifiable alienation, then you have every right to be in their lives. Many participants in the research study I conducted on the long-term effects of PAS on adult-children of divorce (2007) stated that they always hoped that their relationship with their rejected parent would somehow be restored. Dr. Richard A. Warshak, a well-respected expert on PA and PAS, adds that many adult-children he has worked with throughout the years have also stated that they didn't want to be taken seriously nor want the relationship to end in spite of the rejection of a parent (personal communication, February 25, 2011).

If PA rather than PAS is the reason that you have little or no contact with your children, then it may be equally true that every effort needs to be made to repair your relationship with your children. In these cases, it's necessary for you to seek professional help and learn effective ways to overcome the difficulties that caused the parental alienation in the first place. For example, you may need to consider going into rehabilitation to overcome an addiction, take parenting courses, or seek psychotherapy in an effort to create trustworthy and meaningful relationships with your children.

In most PAS cases, you are encouraged to go visit your children at school or meet them somewhere else in the community unless, of course, there is a restraining order or some other court order in place. Show up unexpectedly at their extracurricular events. At least catch a glimpse of them. This will serve the purpose of your children knowing you were there for important events in their lives.

Use Facebook, Twitter, Myspace, YouTube, Flickr, and other types of social networking sources to attempt to let your alienated children know that you are available, that you love and care for them deeply, and want to have a positive relationship with them. Perhaps create your own personal website and show pictures, videos, your children's artwork, past Mother's Day or Father's Day cards, or any other important items or facts to prove that you had a good, loving relationship with your children prior to the alienation. Consider joining online forums to dialogue with other alienated parents and share ideas and personal stories. Consider joining a support group for divorced parents. Become an expert yourself. Help educate the public. Public awareness on PA and PAS is crucial.

... Use Facebook, Twitter, Myspace, YouTube, Flickr, and other types of social networking sources to attempt to let your alienated children know that you are available, that you love and care for them deeply, and want to have a positive relationship with them ...

Be prepared to suggest using child access centers to visit your children. Additionally, be prepared to suggest getting virtual visiting rights in place whether you and your child live in the same locale or not (see Gough, 2006). Many judges throughout the United States and Canada have recently been court ordering virtual visits for use in divorce, custody, PA, and PAS situations. Skype and other types of video conferencing over the Internet are used.

Save money, if possible. Unfortunately, the costs incurred to help reconcile your relationship with your children may get expensive, especially if you're engaged in a child custody and access battle. Although you may run into great expense, please don't despair.

Always remember, especially during difficult times when it seems easier to give up, your children are priceless. You can't place a value on the importance of a healthy, loving relationship with them.

Persistence and perseverance are necessary. Keep in mind, however, that for some individuals there's a fine line between persistence, perseverance, and setting appropriate boundaries versus annoyance, stalking, or criminal harassment. If the latter is something you feel concerned about, talk to a professional such as an attorney or mental health professional who can assist you in sorting out appropriate boundaries.

It's not uncommon to experience consistent failure after making numerous attempts at repairing relationships with alienated children, especially with severe PA and PAS cases. When this happens, many parents question whether it's worthwhile to continue to pursue the relationship or to just give up. This is by no means an easy question to answer. Either way, there are stakes involved. For example, you may choose to pursue the relationship for years but never regain the relationship you were hoping for. Or, you may choose to give up resulting in never seeing your children again. Don't get me wrong—spontaneous reconciliations do occur among some rejected parents and alienated children. The fact is there are no guarantees as each situation is unique.

... It's not uncommon to experience consistent failure after making numerous attempts at repairing relationships with alienated children, especially with severe PA and PAS cases ...

I strongly believe that alienated parents should never give up. In the event that you have made numerous attempts at repairing the relationship yet failure continues to occur, consider perhaps taking a little break to rest and rejuvenate your batteries. Once you feel like your heart, mind, soul, and spirit have filled up and your energy is recouped, try to continue on your journey to attempt to reunify your relationship. Additionally, if you're aware that your child's overall functioning is being affected by various attempts you've been making, then it's a good idea to take a break.

Perhaps at a time like this, you may want to consider using the Serenity Prayer. Depending on your spiritual beliefs, you may want to use alternatives to the word God in the first line with words such as Goddess, Higher Power, Creator, or Universal Force. Hopefully, you will find some sense of peace and serenity in your life no matter what happens in your relationship with your alienated children. ✎

... Hopefully, you will find some sense of peace and serenity in your life no matter what happens in your relationship with your alienated children ...

PART THREE

After the doctoral commencement ceremonies ended,
I finally had time to realize how little I know
and why I need to keep on learning.

Kathleen Reay

Chapter Twenty-Two
Why so Much Controversy?

Although Dr. Richard A. Gardner coined the term "Parental Alienation Syndrome" (PAS) over twenty-five years ago, its recognition has undergone a trickling effect because it remains a complex psycho-legal issue.

Although Dr. Richard A. Gardner coined the term "Parental Alienation Syndrome" (PAS) over twenty-five years ago, its recognition has undergone a trickling effect because it remains a complex psycho-legal issue. The reason appears to be three-fold: First, the PAS theory was developed through Gardner's own personal observations in clinical and forensic practice. Faller (1998, p. 106) pointed out, "Gardner does not provide any research findings to substantiate his assertions about the proposed characteristics and dynamics of the parental alienation syndrome."

... Gardner does not provide any research findings to substantiate his assertions about the proposed characteristics and dynamics of the parental alienation syndrome ...

Second, in a paper presented to various members of the Canadian Senate and the House of Commons who represent the Special Joint Committee on Child Custody and Access, Cartwright (2002, p. 2) stated:

> To some degree, PAS is an artificial problem, promulgated and exacerbated by the adversarial system of child custody dispute adjudication. Seeded by a bad Divorce Act and nurtured by a divorce industry of lawyers, judges, social workers, counselors, psychologists, psychiatrists, and guardians ad litem, it is no surprise that we have harvested a crop of PAS children who see nothing wrong with hurting and rejecting one of their parents out-of-hand, often permanently. (Cartwright, 2002, p. 2).

Third, and perhaps most importantly, there is much debate in the scientific community on whether or not PAS meets criteria necessary to classify it as a valid syndrome. According to the DSM-IV (1994) fourth edition, a syndrome is a "group of symptoms that occur together and that constitute a recognizable condition." Although Gardner argued that PAS is a valid syndrome, characterized by a cluster of eight symptoms that tend to occur together in the child, particularly in the moderate and severe types, several mental health and legal experts maintain that PAS is not a valid syndrome. The latter argument ensues because some empirical and clinical studies demonstrate that not every child who is subject to a parent's alienating behavior will reveal all of the eight manifestations of PAS, as described by Gardner (Bruch, 2001; Dallam, 1999; Emery, 2005; Faller, 1998; Kelly & Johnston, 2001; Williams, 2001). Nonetheless, Gardner (2002b, 2002c) and Warshak (2001) vehemently suggested that the latter is not a persuasive argument to not classify PAS as a valid syndrome. For example, "In medicine, including psychiatry, it is well-recognized that the same pathological agent can produce different outcomes in different individuals. This generally does not invalidate the syndrome or disorder" (Warshak, 2001, p. 38).

Warshak (2001, p. 36) also noted, "To establish the validity of PAS, the scientific literature must demonstrate that the clinical observations that formed the basis for the initial formulation are representative of a wider population of children." He added that scientific validity results from a two-staged process. The first stage begins when other mental health professionals "report on their experiences related to the phenomenon, supplementing and refining the initial proposal" (Warshak, 2001, p. 36). Several scholar practitioners' writings on the psychological characteristics of the alienated child, which are not published in peer-reviewed journals, exemplify the first stage of establishing the validity of PAS (Darnall, 1998; Kopetski, 1998a, 1998b; Stahl, 1999). Other literature relating to the potential long-term effects of PAS also exemplify the first stage process of establishing the validity of PAS (Goldwater, 1991).

...some empirical and clinical studies demonstrate that not every child who is subject to a parent's alienating behavior will reveal all of the eight manifestations of PAS ...

The second stage of establishing the validity of PAS, according to Warshak (2001), occurs when researchers begin to conduct empirical research. He stated "empirical research with larger samples of subjects, standardized and systematic measures, and appropriate scientific controls tests hypotheses drawn from the clinical reports in the literature" (p. 36). Some empirical research has been conducted on the various psychological characteristics of the alienated child (e.g., Burrill, 2001; Moskowitz, 1998; Raso, 2004) and on the long-term consequences of PAS (Baker, 2005a, 2006; Carey, 2003; Raso, 2004; Reay, 2007), which all lend support for the validity of PAS. Clearly, additional research studies need to be conducted on this important topic. This is a serious form of child abuse and constitutes the worst cruelty an alienated parent and child can undergo in toxic divorce situations.

... This is a serious form of child abuse and constitutes the worst cruelty an alienated parent and child can undergo in toxic divorce situations ...

Recently, psychiatrist Dr. William Bernet (2010), submitted, along with a large committee of mental health and legal experts, a proposal to the DSM-V Task Force of the American Psychiatric Association. Rather than making a distinction between PA and PAS as I have discussed in this book, Bernet and his committee propose that the diagnostic term be called "Parental Alienation Disorder" in the upcoming DSM-V under the categories of either a mental disorder or a stand-alone relational problem (Bernet, 2010). Although a parent/child relational problem is presently listed in the DSM-IV-TR (2000), Dr. Bernet and his committee strongly contend that the parental alienation relational problem could be a stand-alone relational problem or at least become a distinct example of a severe parent/child relational problem. Bernet argues that if the DSM-V Task Force of the American Psychiatric Association were to adopt parental alienation as a "mental disorder", then it would be beneficial to list it as Parental Alienation Disorder. He adds, "Parental alienation disorder should be the diagnosis if the child's symptoms are persistent enough and severe enough to meet the criteria for that disorder." Bernet and his colleagues' (2010) proposed diagnostic criteria for Parental Alienation Disorder is outlined below:

Proposed Diagnostic Criteria for Parental Alienation Disorder

A. The child—usually one whose parents are engaged in a high-conflict divorce—allies himself or herself strongly with one parent and rejects a relationship with the other, alienated parent without legitimate justification. The child resists or refuses contact or parenting time with the alienated parent.

B. The child manifests the following behaviors:

- a persistent rejection or denigration of a parent that reaches the level of a campaign;

- weak, frivolous, and absurd rationalizations for the child's persistent criticism of the rejected parent.

C. The child manifests two or more of the following six attitudes and behaviors:

- lack of ambivalence;

- independent-thinker phenomenon;

- reflexive support of one parent against the other;

- absence of guilt over exploitation of the rejected parent;

- presence of borrowed scenarios;

- spread of the animosity to the extended family of the rejected parent.

D. The duration of the disturbance is at least two months.

E. The disturbance causes clinically significant distress or impairment in social, academic (occupational), or other important areas of functioning.

F. The child's refusal to have contact with the rejected parent is without legitimate justification. Parental alienation disorder is not diagnosed if the rejected parent maltreated the child.

... The child—usually one whose parents are engaged in a high-conflict divorce—allies himself or herself strongly with one parent and rejects a relationship with the other, alienated parent without legitimate justification ...

It is important to note that at the time of publishing this book, the outcome of Dr. Bernet and his colleagues' hard work and efforts in advocating for the inclusion of Parental Alienation Disorder in the upcoming DSM-V is still under consideration with the DSM-V Task Force of the American Psychiatric Association (Bernet, presentation, May 28, 2011). It is my belief that the term parental alienation needs to be included in the DSM-V as either a syndrome or a disorder. ⬿

... It is my belief that the term parental alienation needs to be included in the DSM-V as either a syndrome or a disorder ...

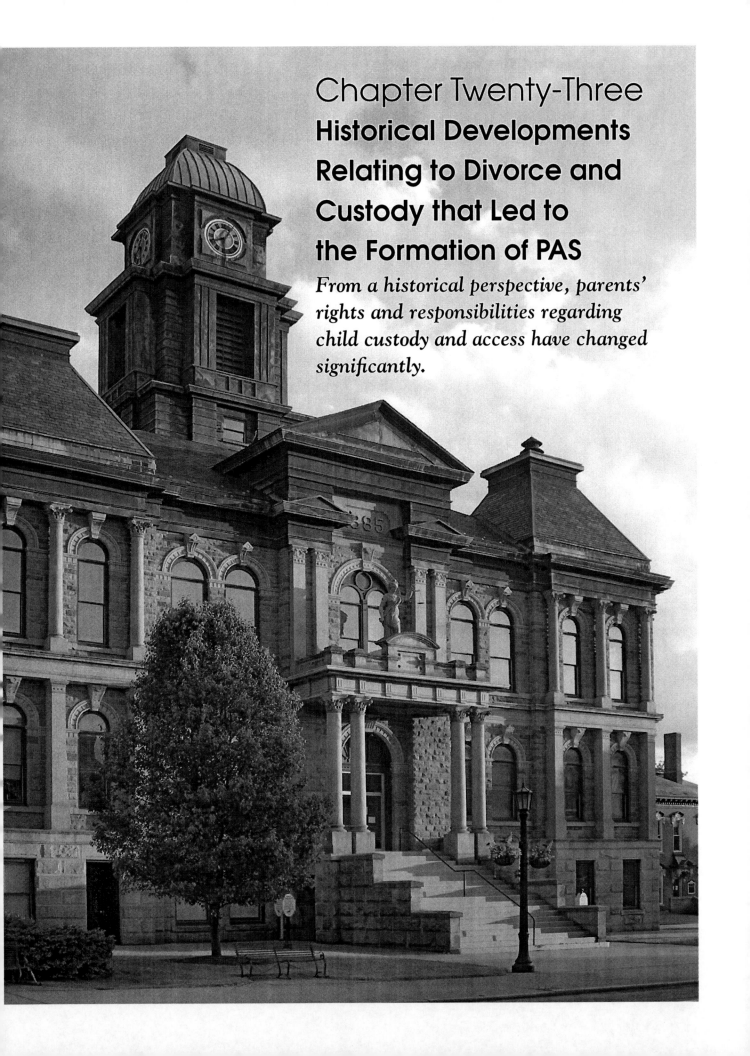

Chapter Twenty-Three

Historical Developments Relating to Divorce and Custody that Led to the Formation of PAS

From a historical perspective, parents' rights and responsibilities regarding child custody and access have changed significantly.

From a historical perspective, parents' rights and responsibilities regarding child custody and access have changed significantly. On the whole, Canadian, American, and British courts have traced their origins to Roman law regarding child custody matters (Boyd, 2003; Derdeyn, 1976; Ellis, 2000; Gardner, 1992a; Warshak, 1992). According to Roman law, paternal bias was deemed appropriate because fathers had complete power and control over their families' lives both pre- and post-divorce. Under the doctrine of 'parens potestas', children were considered property in Roman times. Not only did fathers have the legal rights to support, protect, and educate their children, but they also held the legal rights to sell their children into slavery or murder their children. Throughout the Middle Ages and when English common law was established, children continued to be considered the property of their fathers. Children's needs were not recognized during those times (Boyd, 2003; Derdeyn, 1976; Ellis, 2000; Gardner, 1992a; Warshak, 1992).

Fathers continued to hold custody rights after failed marriages in the mid-nineteenth century. Toward the latter half of the same century, concern for children's welfare during custody disputes began to emerge. After the Norman Conquest of 1066, the doctrine of 'parens potestas' was replaced by the doctrine of 'parens patriae' (Boyd, 2003).

In common law nations, the 'parens patriae' doctrine involved the crown or head of state to assume responsibilities for individuals who

...On the whole, Canadian, American, and British courts have traced their origins to Roman law regarding child custody matters...

were unable to look after their own welfare, which included children and the mentally ill (Boyd, 2003). Further, another responsibility in the same doctrine allowed for a nebulous change in child custody decision-making. That is, legal decisions embarked on recognizing and considering children's needs, rather than recognizing and considering the property rights of fathers. Nonetheless, in the early years of the newly established doctrine, children's best welfare was interpreted as handing over custody rights and responsibilities to the parent who had the financial means to maintain the children's sustenance and material needs. Therefore, in the majority of cases, fathers continued to be granted exclusive custody rights and responsibilities of their children given women held little, if any, economic power and legal rights. Children's rights also remained non-existent.

The effects of the Industrial Revolution, which initiated in Britain and spread throughout the world in the late eighteenth century and the early nineteenth century, began to weaken the patriarchal bias in child custody decision-making (Boyd, 2003). Industrialization brought about critical transformations in the interface of work and family. Gradually, fathers began to seek work away from the family farm or home while wives were expected to support their husbands and children socially, morally, and physically. When wives engaged in wage labor, it was undertaken only so long as they could manage their other job of domestic labor and child care (Burstyn & Smith, 1985).

... Public protests against the injustice of British laws regarding divorce and child custody were just beginning toward the middle of the nineteenth century in Canada ...

Public protests against the injustice of British laws regarding divorce and child custody were just beginning toward the middle of the nineteenth century in Canada (Boyd, 2003; Laing, 1999). First-wave feminists began to confront politicians, judges, and other influential authorities in power about women's inequalities concerning child custody and access (Boyd, 2003). Laing (1999, p. 231) wrote: "Not until 1855, did any Canadian mothers, in cases of widowhood, separation, divorce or abandonment, have even limited legal claim and recourse in regard to their children."

The 'tender years' presumption began to be voiced in Canadian and American legal decision-making in the late nineteenth century and early twentieth century. The tender years doctrine was intended to apply to children under the age of seven or eight who were considered highly dependent on their mothers (Derdeyn, 1976; Gardner, 1992a; Warshak, 1992). Interestingly enough, in English law, the tender years doctrine was originally created to allow divorced mothers temporary custody while breastfeeding their infants. Once breastfeeding ended, it was presumed that children no longer needed to depend on and be in the custody of their mothers. Therefore, the children were returned to their fathers.

... The changing face of child custody decisions truly emerged during the 1920s ...

The changing face of child custody decisions truly emerged during the 1920s. It was at that time that English, Canadian, and American courts of law began to automatically provide custody to mothers rather than fathers (Boyd, 1989a, 1989b, 1989c; Derdeyn, 1976; Warshak, 1992). In the eyes of the law, the tender years presumption became more clear and valued, in spite of the child's age.

Freud's psychoanalytic theory (1949) greatly influenced the conviction that mothers should be given sole custody of their children. Freud stated that the mother's task is "unique ... the first and strongest love object ... the prototype of all later love relations" (p. 90). Further, Bowlby's (1969, 1973) novel theory of attachment and Ainsworth's developmental studies on qualitative differences in attachment (1979, 1989; Ainsworth, Blehar, Waters & Wall, 1978) also greatly influenced the gradual change in maternal custody rights. Under the tender years presumption, the father was unlikely to be granted child custody unless it was proven that the mother was unfit to raise the children (Boyd, 2003; Derdeyn, 1976; Gardner, 1992a).

In 1941, during World War II, divorce rates in Canada nearly tripled from 21.4 divorces per 100,000 married individuals fifteen years of age and over to 63.2 divorces per 100,000 married individuals fifteen years of age and over in 1946 (Mandell & Duffy, 1995). The dramatic increase was largely the consequence of the dissolution of unhappy wartime marriages, those weakened by long separations, and the resulting economic independence acquired by some married women during the war (Mandell & Duffy, 1995).

Canadian divorce rates decreased to 37.7 per 100,000 population in 1951, but steadily rose again between 1952 to 1968 (39.1 to 54.8 per 100,000), and then dramatically after the liberalization of the no fault Divorce Act in the mid 1980s (253.6 per 100,000) (Mandell & Duffy, 1995). In the 1960s, second-wave feminists continued to battle for legislative changes regarding divorce, child custody, and child support reforms (Boyd, 2003). In 1968, Canada's first Divorce Act emerged, which did not alter the tender years presumption. By the end of the 1960s, marital breakdown was becoming a familiar occurrence in Canadian society, and was a factor in the increased labor force participation of women who had to support themselves—and in many cases their dependent children—after their marriages had dissolved. McKie, Prentice, and Reed (1983) reported that husbands were five times less likely to be granted custody of their children compared to wives in 1969.

... In the 1980s, no-fault divorce laws were introduced in both the United States and Canada; it became much easier to obtain a divorce ...

In the 1980s, no-fault divorce laws were introduced in both the United States and Canada; it became much easier to obtain a divorce. Prior to the 1968 Divorce Act in Canada, for example, the only grounds for divorce was proven adultery. Given that a substantial expansion in allowable grounds for divorce occurred in 1968, a large increase in divorces also occurred. The latter seemed to demonstrate that numerous unsatisfactory marriages existed before then but had remained intact because of the stringent divorce laws of the time.

Gardner (1992a) suggested that the enactment of no-fault divorce laws was an important stepping-stone that led to the formation of the PAS. According to him, no-fault divorce laws entailed consensual agreement of both parties but that wasn't always possible. He wrote:

> Divorce can rarely be obtained unilaterally. If one party does not agree, then adversary proceedings are necessary if the person desiring the divorce is to have any hope of getting it. In addition, the new laws have not altered the necessity of resorting to adversary proceedings when there is conflict over such issues as visitation, support, alimony, and custody. Although no-fault divorce laws have considerably reduced the frequency of courtroom conflicts over divorce, litigation over custody is ... very much with us ... [and] on the increase (1992a, p. 52).

... Most courts in the United States substituted the best interests of the child presumption for the tender years presumption in the mid 1970s ...

Besides the enactment of no-fault divorce laws, Gardner (1992a) also argued that two other significant legal system events led to the formation and prevalence of PAS. They were: 1) the complexities surrounding the best interests of the child presumption and 2) the legal concept of joint custody.

Complexities Surrounding the Best Interests of the Child Presumption

Most courts in the United States substituted the best interests of the child presumption for the tender years presumption in the mid 1970s. In Canada, the best interests of the child presumption became prominent in the second Divorce Act, which was declared in 1985. To better appreciate Gardner's argument on how the best interests of the child presumption led to the formation and prevalence of PAS, one needs to begin with a brief glance at some socio-cultural changes that began to emerge in the early 1970s and have continued to present day.

The women's movement in both the United States and Canada

had an enormous influence on the social sciences and the legal systems in the early 1970s (Boyd, 2003; Gardner, 1992a; Stacey and Thorne, 1985). Stacey and Thorne (1985) noted that gender was reconceptualized as a principle of social organization, rather than being viewed as an internal trait or property of individuals. As such, gender and familial norms simultaneously forged. Emerging constructions of gender reflected the diversity of family structure. Various psychological proclivities (for example, men are breadwinners and women are homemakers) altered. Married women increasingly began to contribute to family income outside of the home.

Family law began to be based on the assumptions that women were no more predisposed than men to assume child-care responsibilities, and fathers and mothers were equally capable of parenting. Gardner wrote, "the assumption was made that children's interests would be best served if the courts were 'sex blind' in their ruling on custody disputes" (1992a, p. 53). Therefore, the tender years doctrine that worked in favor of women who were deemed fit mothers was displaced by the gender-neutral best interests of the child doctrine (Boyd, 1989a, 1989b, 1989c, 2003; Gardner, 1992a).

... For the first time in Canadian and American history, children's needs were being put first by family law courts ...

For the first time in Canadian and American history, children's needs were being put first by family law courts. Another interesting occurrence emerged at this point. That was, "fathers who had previously thought that they had no chance of gaining custody found out that they had" (Gardner, 1992a, p. 53). As fathers attempted to obtain child custody based on the best interest of the child presumption, Gardner began to observe some "less noble motives such as vengeance, guilt assuagement, and competition" in the proliferation of child custody litigation battles (p. 53).

The implementation of formal legal equality in family law and social welfare not only failed to end women's structured dependency but also intensified it in some instances upon marital breakdown.

The overall effect of gender-neutral custody law seemed to be that fathers had more power to lay claim to their children than they did prior to the reform (Boyd, 1989a, 1989b). In some instances, for example, the best interests of the child doctrine was equated with the availability of a stay-at-home mother or mother figure. A single mother who engaged in full-time or part-time employment to support her children could easily lose custody to a husband who had a new homemaker-wife, a housekeeper, or some other surrogate mother to look after the children (Boyd, 1989a, 1989b & 1989c). Similarly, a woman could be a full-time mother and still lose custody of her children if she was forced to rely on social welfare and, therefore, live at or below the poverty line (Boyd, 1989a, 1989b & 1989c).

In many cases, courts awarded custody to fathers because it was believed that they could offer a greater standard of living for the children based on their annual net incomes compared to the mothers (Boyd, 1989a, 1989b, & 1989c). Additionally, many mothers could not afford to pay for the services of a qualified, effective lawyer to represent them in high-conflict child custody cases unlike their husbands (Gardner, 1992a). As Boyd (1989a, 1989b, & 1989c) pointed out, the best interests of the child presumption seemed to become equated with economic means and material comfort.

... In many cases, courts awarded custody to fathers because it was believed that they could offer a greater standard of living for the children based on their annual net incomes compared to the mothers ...

Given some of the aforementioned sociocultural, economic, and legal factors, Gardner (1992a) asserted that many mothers had to come up with creative and imaginative ways to build up their justifications for seeking custody of their children. Unfortunately, the children's best interests were not being put to heart. Rather, such creative imagination sometimes became extreme. For instance, it was not uncommon for mothers to make false accusations of child abuse, or sexual abuse against fathers (Gardner, 1992b). The latter also helped fuel the formation of the Parental Alienation Syndrome.

The Legal Concept of Joint Custody

Gardner (1992a) also argued that the legal concept of joint custody, which began in the late 1970s and early 1980s in both the United States and Canada, also led to the formation and prevalence of PAS. According to Gardner (1992a, p. 61), "the notion that one parent be designated the sole custodian and the other the visitor was considered inegalitarian; joint custody promised a more equal division of time with the children and of decision-making powers." Many fathers insisted on playing a larger role in their children's lives after divorce. Most judges during that time frame began to recognize the emergence and demands of men's rights movements in various countries, including the United States and Canada, by handing down judgments based on the suppositions that children needed fathers as much as mothers (Boyd, 1989a, 1989b, & 1989c). Most judges also shared the viewpoint that contemporary men were equally involved in parenting their children (Boyd, 1989b). The "friendly parent" provision in the 1985 Divorce Act of Canada directed courts to operate on the principle that children should have as much contact with each parent as is in their best interests (Boyd, 1989c). Consequently, a small percentage of women were occasionally forced to accept a joint custody arrangement with a spouse who had been physically or sexually abusive (Boyd, 1989c). If she resisted, the mother sometimes lost custody altogether because she was perceived as being uncooperative and/or as putting her own interests before those of the children (Boyd, 1989c).

... In theory or principle, the concept of joint custody is meant to be effective when both parents have the ability to communicate and cooperate effectively with each other as well as to equally share child-rearing roles and responsibilities ...

In theory or principle, the concept of joint custody is meant to be effective when both parents have the ability to communicate and cooperate effectively with each other as well as to equally share child-rearing roles and responsibilities (Gardner, 1992a). Gardner, nonetheless, concluded that the creations of both the legal concept of joint custody and the best interests of the child presumption have ultimately had the effect of making children's custodial arrangements far more unpredictable and precarious. As a result, parents are more frequently brainwashing their children in order to ensure victory in custody/visitation litigation. And the children themselves have joined forces with the preferred parent in order to preserve what they consider to be the most desirable arrangement, without the appreciation that in some cases primary custody by the denigrated parent might be in their best interests (Gardner, 1992a, p. 61-62).

Although Gardner observed children at various ages being programmed or brainwashed by one parent against the other prior to the early 1980s, he saw with increasing frequency a new phenomenon primarily in children who had been entangled in protracted custody litigation (1985, 1992a). For that reason, he coined the term Parental Alienation Syndrome. With the burgeoning phenomenon of PAS in present time, judicial determinations of custody based on the notion of equal parenting and justified by what is best for children in many ways has worked to the disadvantage of some mothers, fathers, and children. It's quite likely that the second-wave feminists who vehemently critiqued the old paternalistic divorce statutes and relentlessly pressed for family law reform to implement formal legal equality did not anticipate such an outcome.

... With the burgeoning phenomenon of PAS in present time, judicial determinations of custody based on the notion of equal parenting and justified by what is best for children in many ways has worked to the disadvantage of some mothers, fathers, and children ...

Time for Self-Reflection

What were the most significant things you learned from reading this chapter?

_____

_____

_____

_____

_____

_____

_____

_____

_____

_____

_____

_____

_____

_____

_____

_____

_____

_____

_____

_____

_____

_____

_____

_____

_____

_____

Chapter Twenty-Four
Special Considerations for Counseling Alienated Parents

Mental health professionals who choose to work with this particular population require specialized training, clinical supervision, and experience.

...Some self-referred alienated parents may be able to bring their children in for family therapy; however, most are not able to ...

Very often, a third-party such as a judge or attorney, or alienated parents themselves, request the services of a mental health professional for individual and/or family counseling. When this occurs, the targeted parents may have some contact with their children while others may not. Some self-referred alienated parents may be able to bring their children in for family therapy; however, most are not able to. In the latter situations, the children not only refuse to attend family therapy but their alienating parents dissuade and discourage them from taking part in it. Still those alienated parents who do maintain some form of contact with their children often endure a lot of hostility, rejection, and other negative behaviors from their children before, during, or after the therapy sessions. In some instances, alienated parents may have been awarded restored visiting rights by the courts after a brief, medium, or long absence from seeing their children. Sometimes this works and sometimes it doesn't. There are numerous other hurdles and obstacles that can also get in the way for alienated parents in an attempt to rebuild their relationships with their children. All in all, not only are the varying dynamics involved very challenging and difficult for the alienated parent, but it is often very challenging and difficult for the clinician to work with.

Mental health professionals who choose to work with this particular population require specialized training, clinical supervision, and experience. From an ethical perspective, competency in being able to work with this particular population is pertinent. Otherwise, the particular members of an alienated family that you work with may potentially endure some type of harm even though that was never your intention. Sadly but true, some therapists have made errors that resulted in the perpetuation of the alienation or even inadvertently created the total loss and demise of a child's relationship with the rejected parent. Clearly, all clinicians have an ethical duty to protect children from harm. Nonetheless, when therapists have a lack of knowledge and understanding of PAS or lack the experience in identifying and recognizing the level of severity of PAS, the alienated child could undergo more harm than good for a lifetime. With severe PAS, obsessive alienators are entrenched in their own irrational and delusional belief system and will not listen to reason from anyone—including professionals. In these cases, the alienated children need to be removed from the alienating parent's care through legal intervention. If you currently lack the required knowledge and understanding of PAS or are inexperienced with PAS, please don't feel reluctant, afraid, or ashamed to refer the client to another clinician who is well qualified and experienced with PA or PAS cases. It's not worth taking the risk not to refer if you feel you are not properly qualified to help a member of an alienated family.

> *... Clearly, all clinicians have an ethical duty to protect children from harm ...*

Clinicians who work with this particular population must be willing and able to muster a lot of extra patience, understanding, empathy, devotion, and other important clinical strengths and means. In doing this type of work, you must also be willing and available to write reports for legal professionals and the courts as well as attend court. You need to keep abreast of up-to-date research findings and legal issues pertaining to PA and PAS. When working with this particular population, compassion fatigue among therapists is not uncommon. The practice of personal and professional boundary setting as well as self-care is essential to help avoid clinician burnout.

In true cases of PAS, one of the most important things to keep in mind when working with alienated parents is that what they are experiencing is real and must not be discounted by any means. Being non-judgmental at all times is paramount. Validation and strengthening of the alienated parent's worth as a parent is essential. Utilizing a strengths-based focus is very helpful.

Generally speaking, most alienated parents' goals for individual therapy involve learning skills to manage hurt, anxiety, fear, panic, depression, grief, loss, anger, stress, and shame. In some instances, you will find they are also reaching out for other types of help such as overcoming addictive behaviors. You may also come across some rejected parents who are suicidal and need immediate interventions. Unfortunately, but true, there are reported cases of alienated parents who have threatened or committed suicide (Cross, 2000; Johnston & Roseby, 1997; Smith, 1991; Warshak, 2003).

... Depending on the situation, some alienated parents may need effective parent-child communication skills and other types of parenting skills to help boost their confidence and offset any suspected or disclosed areas at risk which may prevent the parent-child relationship from being reestablished ...

Depending on the situation, some alienated parents may need effective parent-child communication skills and other types of parenting skills to help boost their confidence and offset any suspected or disclosed areas at risk which may prevent the parent-child relationship from being reestablished. Many rejected parents that I've had the pleasure of working with are eager to learn about various aspects of child and youth development. Given they are working hard toward having a meaningful relationship with their children and clearly wanting to do what is in their child's best interests, they appreciate receiving insights into children's needs. In certain situations, alienated parents may also require effective skills for working toward a reasonable relationship with the other parent.

Many parents require trauma therapy to help soothe the pain and anguish associated with being alienated. Professionally, I have found that traditional forms of trauma therapy, CBT, solution-focused interventions, and Eye Movement Desensitization and Reprocessing

(EMDR) therapy have been helpful for rejected parents who have been significantly traumatized.

Many targeted parents also require psycho-educational guidance with respect to the nature of the court system. For example, alienated parents commonly complain, feel extremely frustrated, anxious, and confused over the length of time it takes to go to court to gain visiting and custody rights. It's not uncommon for courts to adjourn, which also causes frustration and annoyance for targeted parents. Some alienating parents fire lawyers or lawyers fire them creating more complexities including prolonging the process. The entire adversarial system in family courts can be a very overwhelming tribulation for alienated parents.

Why Incorporate a CBT Approach with Alienated Parents?

Some mental health professionals who read this workbook may wonder why I chose to emphasize a cognitive-behavioral therapy (CBT) approach rather than other therapeutic modalities. Perhaps it may make more sense to you that CBT should be offered to alienating parents and alienated children rather than to rejected parents. The answer is cognitive theory and research has shown that cognitive distortions in patients contribute to a number of psychological and behavioral disorders (Beck, 1976; Beck et al., 2004; Millon & Davis, 1996). In the mid 70s, Aaron Beck found a positive correlation between cognitive distortions and pathology associated with psychological and behavioral factors (1976). His theory serves as a significant basis of cognitive therapy given emotion and behavior are immensely influenced by cognition. Beck also acknowledged important similarities between behavior therapy and cognitive therapy and the fact that both therapies act directly on the symptoms that create distress. Not only is there widespread recognition that distorted or maladaptive cognitions play a prominent role in the etiology of psychological distress, but there is also

... Many targeted parents also require psycho-educational guidance with respect to the nature of the court system. For example, alienated parents commonly complain, feel extremely frustrated, anxious, and confused over the length of time it takes to go to court to gain visiting and custody rights ...

widespread recognition that distorted or maladaptive cognitions play a prominent role in the perpetuation of psychological distress (Beck et al., 2004; Dobson & Dozois, 2001). Moreover, the value of shifting cognitive distortions is reinforced by empirical reports suggesting that the influence of negative life events on subjective feelings is much more powerful than that of positive life events (Larsen & Prizmic, 2004). The reformulation of the learned helplessness model of depression suggests that the tendency toward internal, stable, and global explanations for negative events increases the risk of depression (Seligman et al., 1988).

CBT has been extensively used for treating depression; anxiety disorders such as panic disorder and agoraphobia, social phobia, post-traumatic stress, obsessive-compulsive disorder; eating disorders; addictive disorders; certain chronic illnesses; personality disorders; and some forms of psychoses (Beck, 1993; J. Beck, 1998; Eimer, 1989; Young, 2002; Walker, 2004). As previously mentioned, many alienated parents that you will see in clinical settings experience one or more types of psychological distress such as grief, helplessness, hopelessness, depression, acute or chronic stress, anxiety, fear, worry, panic, low tolerance for frustrating and difficult situations, anger, post-traumatic stress, and addiction among other types. Thus, the overwhelming body of literature reviews on the efficacy of CBT as a therapeutic approach for treating various types of psychological distress, including relationship difficulties, lends support for treating not only alienating parents but alienated parents and children, too.

One of the beauties of utilizing CBT is that the synthesis of cognitive and behavioral techniques forms a package that can be tailored to the needs of an alienated family. As an example, interventions for alienated parents diagnosed with mood disorders, anxiety disorders, addictive disorders, and/or medical illnesses need to emphasize coping skills, problem-solving strategies, and cognitive

... CBT has been extensively used for treating depression; anxiety disorders such as panic disorder and agoraphobia, social phobia, post-traumatic stress, obsessive-compulsive disorder; eating disorders; addictive disorders; certain chronic illnesses; personality disorders; and some forms of psychoses ...

restructuring. Obviously, a mental health professional will utilize a repertoire of skills and strategies to fit specific client needs.

With alienated parents, it is especially important to promote a sense of empowerment to help offset the pain and anguish they experience. Self-efficacy theory is based on the recognition that human beings have an intrinsic need to feel competent in order to attain their desired goals (Bandura, 1997). Various behavioral techniques offered to the client can help promote the development of self-efficacy.

It is beneficial to use CBT to help rejected parents identify and challenge various types of counterproductive thinking such as assumptions of being a bad parent, being inadequate, lacking self-trust, lacking judgment of self and others, vulnerability, helplessness, and a never ending pattern of defeat. Multifaceted CBT interventions that draw on a variety of strategies and techniques to alter distorted cognitions and facilitate certain types of behavioral change can be beneficial.

... Multifaceted CBT interventions that draw on a variety of strategies and techniques to alter distorted cognitions and facilitate certain types of behavioral change can be beneficial ...

As part of the therapeutic process, the alienated parent learns to recognize, monitor, and record counterproductive thinking in a journal or can use a more structured format such as a daily thought record (see Burns). Journal keeping, self-monitoring, completing homework assignments, and providing the therapist with feedback are useful strategies. Throughout the CBT journey, the alienated client is able to shift his or her information processing from a maladaptive to an adaptive level. In doing so, the client's self-concept, self-esteem, and overall sense of functioning can greatly improve. All in all, CBT is very complimentary to use with other therapeutic approaches such as Humanistic, Existential, Psychodynamic, Interpersonal, Solution-Focused, and Eye Movement Desensitization and Reprocessing (EMDR).

Thank you for your interest in this workbook. I hope it helps increase the effectiveness of the clinical services you choose to offer. Working with individuals and/or families suffering from the effects of parental alienation can be a very gratifying experience when good work is done by all parties involved to repair the parent-child relationship. I offer you sincere gratitude for choosing to work with this very special population. This genuinely makes you a very special person. You are making a valuable contribution to the well-being of many individuals and families. ❧

... Working with individuals and/or families suffering from the effects of parental alienation can be a very gratifying experience when good work is done by all parties involved to repair the parent-child relationship ...

An Adapted Version of the Serenity Prayer

God, Goddess, Creator, my Higher Power or Universal Force,

grant me the serenity

to accept the things I cannot change,

the courage to change the things I can,

and the wisdom to know the difference.

Original by Reinhold Niebuhr

Epilogue

Facing the reality of parental alienation or parental alienation syndrome is a painful and difficult journey for both alienated parents and their children. I encourage each and every rejected parent to please not wait until the situation between you and your child becomes bad. Reach out for help as soon as possible. This workbook will hopefully offer you greater understanding, hope, self-esteem, and strategies to cope and function as effectively as possible.

If you have been fortunate enough to have reconciled with your child, then hopefully you are each other's greatest allies. If you are still traveling this road alone, please don't despair. Hopefully, this book will help you find ways to make your life more rewarding no matter what happens in the future. Even though recovery from being an alienated parent will be an ongoing process, this doesn't mean that you won't be rewarded for your efforts all along the way.

I would be very grateful hearing how this book has affected you. Please feel free to email me at drkathleenreay@gmail.com or write to Suite 204 – 74 Wade Ave., E., Penticton, British Columbia, Canada, V2A 8M4.

I wish you the very best.

About the Author

Kathleen M. Reay, Ph.D. is a researcher, author, public speaker, litigation-related consultant, and licensed psychotherapist in private practice specializing in parental alienation syndrome. She was honored to achieve Diplomate status with the American Academy of Experts in Traumatic Stress in collaboration with the National Center for Crisis Management, Washington, D.C. Dr. Reay is also a full-time member of the American Psychological Association, the Canadian Psychological Association, EMDR Canada, EMDRIA US, and the B.C. Association of Clinical Counselors. She was a keynote speaker at the 2011 Canadian Symposium for Parental Alienation Syndrome in Montreal, Quebec. Dr. Reay is a well-loved speaker whose practical ideas, wealth of experience, and great sense of humor make her seminars both valuable and enjoyable. She has been a guest speaker on Vancouver radio talk shows and has appeared on a major Canadian television network in a parent education program. Her work has also been featured in regional newspapers and a nation-wide parent educators' magazine. She has been happily married to the same man for over 30 years, has two adult daughters, a beautiful new grandson, two yellow Labradors, and a kitten.

Dr. Reay can be reached at 250.276.9467. You can email her at drkathleenreay@gmail.com or visit her website at http://www.parentalalienationhelp.org

References

Ainsworth, M. (1979). Attachment as related to mother-infant interaction. In J. S. Rosenblatt, R. A. Hinde, C. Beer, & M. Busnel (Eds.), *Advances in the study of behavior* (pp. 159-228). New York: Academic Press.

Ainsworth, M. (1989). Attachments beyond infancy. *American Psychologist, 44,* 709-716.

Ainsworth, M., Blehar, M., Waters, E., & Wall, S. (1978). *Patterns of attachment: A psychological study of the strange situation.* Hillsdale, NJ: Erlbaum.

Amato, P. (1993). Children's adjustment to divorce: Theories, hypotheses, and empirical support. *Journal of Marriage and the Family, 55,* 23-38.

Amato, P. (1994). Life-span adjustment of children to their parents' divorce. *The Future of Children: Children and Divorce, 4,* 143-164.

Amato, P. (1996). Explaining the intergenerational transmission of divorce. *Journal of Marriage and the Family, 58,* 628-640.

Amato, P., & Keith, B. (1991a). Parental divorce and the well-being of children: A meta-analysis. *Psychological Bulletin, 110,* 26-46.

Amato, P., & Keith, B. (1991b). Parental divorce and adult well-being: A meta-analysis. *Journal of Marriage and Family, 53,* 43-58.

American Psychiatric Association (1994). *Diagnostic and statistical manual of mental disorders* (4th ed.). Washington, DC: American Psychiatric Association.

American Psychiatric Association. (2000). *Diagnostic and statistical manual of mental disorders* (4th ed., text revision). Washington, DC: American Psychiatric Association.

Andritzky, W. (2006). The role of medical reports in the development of parental alienation syndrome. In R. A. Gardner, S. R. Sauber, & D. Lorandos (Eds.), *The international handbook of parental alienation syndrome: Conceptual, clinical and legal considerations* (pp. 195-208). Springfield, IL: Charles C. Thomas Publisher, Ltd.

Baker, A. J. L. (2005a). The long-term effects of parental alienation on adult children: A qualitative research study. *American Journal of Family Therapy, 33,* 289-302.

Baker, A. J. L. (2005b). The cult of parenthood: A qualitative study of parental alienation. *Cultic Studies Review, 4,* 1-19.

Baker, A. J. L. (2006). Patterns of parental alienation syndrome: A qualitative study of adults who were alienated from a parent as a child. *American Journal of Family Therapy, 34,* 63-78.

Baker, A.J. L. (2007a). Knowledge and attitudes about the parental alienation syndrome: A survey of custody evaluators. *American Journal of Family Therapy, 35,* 1-19.

Baker, A. J. L. (2007b). *Adult Children of Parental Alienation Syndrome: Breaking the Ties that Bind.* New York: W.W. Norton.

Bandura, A. (1997). *Self-efficacy: The exercise of control.* New York: Freeman.

B.C. court bars mother from seeing daughter for more than a year. (2009, March 9). *The Canadian Press.* Retrieved from http://www. winnipegfreepress.com.

Beck, A. T. (1967). *Depression: Clinical, experimental, and theoretical aspects.* New York: Harper & Row.

Beck, A.T. (1976). *Cognitive therapy and the emotional disorders.* New York: International Universities Press.

Beck, A. T. (1993). Cognitive therapy: Past, present, and future. *Journal of Consulting and Clinical Psychology,* 61, 194-198.

Beck, A. T., & Emery, G., with Greenberg, R. L. (1985). *Anxiety disorders and phobias: A cognitive perspective.* New York: Basic Books.

Beck, A.T., Freeman, A., Davis, D.D., & Associates (2004). *Cognitive Therapy of Personality Disorders* (2nd ed.). New York: Guilford Press.

Beck, A.T., & Weishaar, M.E. (1989). Cognitive therapy. In A. Freeman, K.M. Simon, L.E. Beutler, & H. Arkowitz (Eds.), *Comprehensive handbook of cognitive therapy* (pp. 21-36). New York: Plenum Press.

Beck, J.S. (1998). *Complex cognitive therapy treatment for personality disorder patients.* Bulletin of the Menninger Clinic, 62,170-194.

Bernet, W. (2010). *Parental alienation, DSM-5, and ICD-11.* Springfield, IL: Charles C. Thomas Publisher, Ltd.

Bernet, W. (2011, May). *The differential diagnosis of contact refusal.* Speech presented at the Canadian Symposium for Parental Alienation Syndrome, Montreal, Quebec.

Berns, S. (2006). Recognition of PAS in Australia. In R.A. Gardner, S. R. Sauber, & D. Lorandos (Eds.), *The international handbook of parental alienation syndrome: Conceptual, clinical and legal considerations* (pp. 121-130). Springfield, IL: Charles C. Thomas Publisher, Ltd.

Bow, J.N., Gould, J.W., & Flens, J.R. (2009). Examining parental alienation in child custody cases: A survey of mental health and legal professionals. *American Journal of Family Therapy, 37,* 127-145.

Bowlby, J. (1969*). Attachment and Loss: Volume I. Attachment.* New York: Basic Books.

Bowlby, J. (1973). *Attachment and Loss: Volume II. Separation.* New York: Basic Books.

Boyd, S. (1989a). Child custody, ideologies and employment. *Canadian Journal of Women and the Law, 3,* 111-33.

Boyd, S. (1989b). From gender-specificity to gender-neutrality? Ideologies in Canadian child custody law. In C. Smart & S. Sevenhuijsen (Eds.), *Child custody and the politics of gender* (pp. 126-157). London: Routledge.

Boyd, S. (1989c). Child custody law and the invisibility of women's work. *Queen's Quarterly, 96,* 831-858.

Boyd, S. (2003). *Child custody, law, and women's work.* Toronto: Oxford University Press. Braver, S., Ellman, I., & Fabricius, W. (2003). Relocation of children after divorce and children's best interests: New evidence and legal considerations. *Journal of Family Psychology, 17,* 206-219.

Braver, S., Ellman, I., & Fabricius, W. (2003). Relocation of children after divorce and children's best interests: New evidence and legal considerations. *Journal of Family Psychology, 17,* 206-219.

Bruch, C. (2001). Parental alienation syndrome and parental alienation: Getting it wrong in child custody cases. *Family Law Quarterly, 35,* 527-552.

Burns, D.M. (1999). *Feeling good: The new mood therapy.* New York: Harper Collins Publishers, Inc.

Burrill, J. (2001). Parental alienation syndrome in court referred custody cases (Doctoral dissertation). Retrieved April 5, 2006, from http://dissertation. com/library/1121490a.htm

Burrill, J. (2006). Descriptive statistics of the mild, moderate, and severe characteristics of parental alienation syndrome. In R. A. Gardner, S. R. Sauber, & D. Lorandos (Eds.), *The international handbook of parental alienation syndrome: Conceptual, clinical and legal considerations* (pp. 49-55). Springfield, IL: Charles C. Thomas Publisher, Ltd.

Burstyn, V., & Smith, D. (1985). *Women, class, family and the state.* Toronto: Garamond.

Carey, K. (2003). Exploring long-term outcomes of the parental alienation syndrome (Doctoral dissertation). *ProQuest Information and Learning Company,* (UMI,3088909).

Cartwright, G. (1993). Expanding the parameters of parental alienation syndrome. *American Journal of Family Therapy, 21,* 205- 215.

Cartwright, G. (2002). *The changing face of parental alienation syndrome.* Retrieved August 28, 2006, from http://www.education.mcgill.ca/pain/changingface.htm

Clawar, S., & Rivlin, S. (1991). C*hildren held hostage: Dealing with programmed and brainwashed children.* Chicago: American Bar Association.

Cross, P. (2000). *Lost children: A guide for separating parents.* London: Velvet Glove Publishing.

Dallam, S. (1999). *Parental alienation syndrome: Is it scientific?* Retrieved April 16, 2006, from http://www.leadershipcouncil.org/1/res/Dallam/3.html

Darnall, D. (1997). *Three types of parental alienation.* Retrieved October 22, 2005, from http://www.parentalalienation.com/PASfound1.htm

Darnall, D. (1998). *Divorce casualties: Protecting your children from parental alienation.* Lanham, MD: Taylor Trade Publishing.

Darnall, D. (2010). *Beyond divorce casualties: Reunifying the alienated family.* Lanham, MD: Taylor Trade Publishing.

Darnall, D. (2011, May). *The psychosocial treatment of parental alienation.* Speech presented at the Canadian Symposium for Parental Alienation Syndrome, Montreal, Quebec.

Derdeyn, A. (1976). Child custody contests in historical perspective. *American Journal of Psychiatry, 133,* 1369-1376.

Dobson, K.S., & Dozois, D.J.A. (2001). Historical and philosophical bases of the cognitive-behavioral therapies. In K.S. Dobson (Ed.), *Handbook of cognitive behavioral therapies* (pp. 3-39). New York: Guilford Press.

Dunne, J., & Hedrick, M. (1994). The parental alienation syndrome: An analysis of sixteen selected cases. *Journal of Divorce & Remarriage, 21,* 21-37.

Duryee, M. (1992). Mandatory court mediation: Demographic summary and consumer evaluation of one court service. *Family & Conciliation Courts Review, 30,* 260-267.

Eimer, B.N. (1989). Psychotherapy for chronic pain: A cognitive approach. In A. Freeman, K.M. Simon, L.E. Beutler, & H. Arkowitz (Eds.), *Comprehensive handbook of cognitive therapy* (pp. 449-465). New York: Plenum Press.

Ellis, A. (1957). Rational psychotherapy and individual psychology. *Journal of Individual Psychology, 13,* 38-44.

Ellis, E. (2000). Parental alienation syndrome: A new challenge for family courts. In E.M. Ellis (Ed.), *Divorce wars: Interventions with families in conflict* (pp. 205-233). Washington: American Psychological Association.

Emery, R. (2005). Parental alienation syndrome: Proponents bear the burden of proof. *Family Court Review, 43,* 8-13.

Faller, K. (1998). The parental alienation syndrome: What is it and what data support it? *Child Maltreatment, 3,* 100-115.

Family Conflict Resolution Services (2006). *Understanding and effectively dealing with hostile-aggressive parenting (HAP).* Oakville, Ont.: Family Conflict Resolution Services.

Franklin, K., Janoff-Bulman, R., & Roberts, J. (1990). Long-term impact of parental divorce on optimism and trust: Changes in general assumptions or narrow beliefs? *Journal of Personality and Social Psychology, 59,* 743-755.

Freud, S. (1949). *An outline of psychoanalysis*. New York: W.W. Norton.

Garber, B.D. (2004). Therapist alienation: Foreseeing and forestalling dynamics undermining therapies with children. *Professional Psychology: Research and Practice, 35(4)*, 357-363.

Gardner, R. (1985). Recent trends in divorce and custody litigation. *Academy Forum, 29*, 3-7.

Gardner, R. (1987). *The parental alienation syndrome and the differentiation between fabricated and genuine child sex abuse*. Cresskill, NJ: Creative Therapeutics.

Gardner, R. (1992a). *The parental alienation syndrome: A guide for mental health and legal professionals*. Cresskill, NJ: Creative Therapeutics.

Gardner, R. (1992b). *True and false accusations of child sex abuse*. Cresskill, NJ: Creative Therapeutics.

Gardner, R. (1994). Differentiating between true and false sex-abuse accusations in child custody disputes. *Journal of Divorce and Remarriage, 21*, 1-20.

Gardner, R. (1998a). *The parental alienation syndrome*. Cresskill, NJ: Creative Therapeutics.

Gardner, R. (1998b). Recommendations for dealing with parents who induce a parental alienation syndrome in their children. *Journal of Divorce & Remarriage, 28*, 1-23.

Gardner, R. (2001). Should courts order PAS children to visit/reside with the alienated parent? A follow-up study. *American Journal of Forensic Psychology, 19*, 61-106.

Gardner, R. (2002a). *PAS and the DSM-V: A call for action*. Retrieved November 20, 2005, from http://mensnewsdaily.com/archive/g/gardner/gardner100602.htm

Gardner, R. (2002b). Misinformation versus facts about the contributions of Richard A. Gardner, M.D. *American Journal of Family Therapy, 30*, 395-416.

Gardner, R. (2002c). *Misinformation versus facts about the contributions of Richard A. Gardner, M.D.: May 2002 Revision*. Retrieved April 16, 2006, from http://www.rgardner.com/refs/misperceptions_versus_facts.html

Gardner, R. (2002d). Parental alienation syndrome vs. parental alienation: Which diagnosis should evaluators use in child custody disputes? *American Journal of Family Therapy, 30,* 93-115.

Gardner, R. (2003). Court rulings specifically recognizing the parental alienation syndrome in the US and Internationally. Retrieved August 21, 2006, from http://www.rgardner.com/refs/pas_legalcities.html

Gardner, R. (2006). Chapter 1 introduction. In R. A. Gardner, S. R. Sauber, & & D. Lorandos (Eds.), *The international handbook of parental alienation syndrome: Conceptual, clinical and legal considerations* (pp. 5-11). Springfield, IL: Charles C. Thomas Publisher, Ltd.

Garrity, C., & Baris, M. (1994). *Caught in the middle: Protecting the children of high conflict divorce.* Lexington, MA: Lexington Books.

Glenn, N., & Kramer, K. (1985). The psychological well-being of adult children of divorce. *Journal of Marriage & the Family, 47,* 905-912.

Glenn, N., & Kramer, K. (1987). The marriages and divorces of the children of divorce. *Journal of Marriage & the Family, 49,* 811-825.

Glenn, N., & Shelton, B. (1983). Pre-adult background variables and divorce. *Journal of Marriage & the Family, 45,* 405-410.

Goldwater, A. (1991). Le syndrome d'aliénation parentale (in English). In *Développements récents en droit familial* (pp. 121-145). Cowansville, Que.: Les Iditions Yvon Blais.

Gottlieb, D. (2006). Parental alienation syndrome - An Israeli perspective: Reflections and recommendations. In R.A. Gardner, S. R. Sauber, & D. Lorandos (Eds.), *The international handbook of parental alienation syndrome: Conceptual, clinical and legal considerations* (pp. 90-107). Springfield, IL: Charles C. Thomas Publisher, Ltd.

Gottman, J. M., & Silver, N. (1999). *The seven principles for making marriage work: A practical guide from the country's foremost relationship expert.* New York: Three Rivers Press.

Gough, M. (2006). *Video Conferencing Over IP: Configure, Secure, and Troubleshoot.* Rockland, MA.: Syngress Publishing, Inc.

Haddad, T. (1998). Do children in post-divorce custody have more problems than those in intact families? (Workshop paper prepared for a National Research Conference, Investing in Children, October 27-29,

1998, Ottawa). Based on Tony Haddad, *Custody Arrangements and the Emotional or Behavioural Problems of Children*. Ottawa: Human Resources Development Canada, 1998 (W-98-9E, pp. 1-8).

Hays, K. F. (1999). *Working it out: Using exercise in psychotherapy*. Washington, DC: American Psychological Association.

Hetherington, E. M. (1989). Coping with family transitions: Winners, losers, and survivors. *Child Development, 60*, 1-14.

Hetherington, E. M., Cox, M., & Cox, R. (1985). Long-term effects of divorce and remarriage on the adjustment of children. *Journal of the American Academy of Child Psychiatry, 24*, 518-530.

Hetherington, E. M., Stanley-Hagan, M., & Anderson, E. (1989). Marital transitions: A child's perspective. *American Psychologist, 44*, 303-312.

Hobbs, T. (2006). Legal requirements of experts giving evidence to courts in the United Kingdom: PAS and the experts' failure to comply. In R.A. Gardner, S. R. Sauber, & D. Lorandos (Eds.), *The international handbook of parental alienation syndrome: Conceptual, clinical and legal considerations* (pp. 439-449). Springfield, IL: Charles C. Thomas Publisher, Ltd.

Jacobson, D. (1978). The impact of marital separation/divorce on children: II. Interpersonal hostility and child adjustment. *Journal of Divorce, 2*, 3-19.

Johnston, J. (1993). Children of divorce who refuse visitation. In C. Depner and J. H. Bray (Eds.), *Non-residential parenting: New vistas in family living*, pages 109-135. Newbury Park, California: Sage.

Johnston, J. (2003). Parental alignments and rejection: An empirical study of alienation in children of divorce. *Journal of the American Academy of Psychiatry and the Law, 31*, 158-170.

Johnston, J. (2005). Children of divorce who reject a parent and refuse visitation: Recent research and social policy implications for the alienated child. *Family Law Quarterly, 38*, 757-775.

Johnston, J., & Campbell, L. (1988). *Impasses of divorce: The dynamics and resolution of family conflict*. New York: Free Press.

Johnston, J., Campbell, L., & Mayers, S. (1985). Latency children in post separation and divorce disputes. *Journal of the American Academy of Child Psychiatry, 24*, 563-574.

Johnston, J., & Roseby, V. (1997). *In the name of the child.* New York: Simon & Schuster, Inc.

Kalter, N., Kioner, A., Schreier, S., & Okla, M. (1989). Predictors of children's post divorce adjustment. *American Journal of Orthopsychiatry, 59,* 605-618.

Kelly, J., & Johnston, J. (2001). The alienated child: A reformulation of parental alienation syndrome. *Family Court Review, 39,* 249-266.

Kopetski, L. (1998a). Identifying cases of parent alienation syndrome - Part I. *Colorado Lawyer,* February, 27, 65-68. Retrieved April 8, 2006, from http://www.fact.on.ca/Info/pas/kopet98a.htm

Kopetski, L. (1998b). Identifying cases of parent alienation syndrome - Part II. *Colorado Lawyer,* March, 27, 63-66. Retrieved April 8, 2006, from http://www.fact.on.ca/Info/pas/kopet98b.htm

Kübler-Ross, E. (1969). *On death and dying: What the dying have to teach doctors, nurses, clergy, and their own families.* New York: Touchstone.

Kulka, R., & Weingarten, H. (1979). The long-term effects of parental divorce in childhood on adult adjustment. *Journal of Social Issues, 35,* 50-78.

Kurdek, L., & Siesky, A. (1980). Children's perceptions of their parents' divorce. *Journal of Divorce, 3,* 339-378.

Kurdek, L., & Siesky, A. (1981). Effects of divorce on children: The relationship between parent and child perspectives. *Journal of Divorce, 4,* 85-99.

Laing, M. (1999). For the sake of the children: Preventing reckless new laws. *Canadian Journal of Family Law, 16,* 229-283.

Lampel, A. (1996). Children's alignment with parents in highly conflicted custody cases. *Family and Conciliation Courts Review, 34,* 229-239.

Larsen, R.K. & Prizmic, Z. (2004). Affect regulation. In RF. Baumeister & K.D. Vohs (Eds.), *Handbook of self-regulation: Research, theory and applications* (pp. 40-61). New York: Guilford Press.

Leitner, W., & Kunneth, A. (2006). Parental alienation syndrome: Theory and practice in Germany. In R.A. Gardner, S. R. Sauber, & D. Lorandos (Eds.), *The international handbook of parental alienation syndrome: Conceptual, clinical and legal considerations* (pp. 108-120). Springfield, IL: Charles C. Thomas Publisher, Ltd.

Lenzenweger, M.F., Lane, M. C., Loranger, A.W. & Kessler, R.C. (2007). DSM-IV personality disorders in the national comorbidity survey replication. *Biological Psychiatry, 15,* 553-64.

Lipman, E., Offord, D., & Dooley, M. (1996). What do we know about children from single-mother families? In: *Growing Up in Canada: National Longitudinal Survey of Children and Youth.* Ottawa: Human Resources Development Canada, Statistics Canada (Catalogue No. 89-550-MPE).

Lowenstein, L. (2006). The psychological effects and treatment of the parental alienation syndrome. In R.A. Gardner, S. R. Sauber, & D. Lorandos (Eds.), *The international handbook of parental alienation syndrome: Conceptual, clinical and legal considerations* (pp. 292-301). Springfield, IL: Charles C. Thomas Publisher, Ltd.

Lund, M. (1992). *Mediation: Parental alienation syndrome.* Retrieved August 12, 2004, from http://www.fact.on.ca/Info/pas/lund92.htm

Lund, M. (1995). A therapist's view of parental alienation syndrome. *Family and Conciliation Courts Review, 33,* 308-316.

Maccoby, E., & Mnookin, R. (1992). *Dividing the child: Social and legal dilemmas of custody.* Cambridge, Massachusetts: Harvard University Press.

Machuca, L. (2005). Parental alienation syndrome: Perceptions of parental behaviors and attitudes in divorced vs. non-divorced families. (master's thesis). *Proquest Information and Learning Company,* (UMI, 1430453).

Major, J. A. (2000). *Parents who have successfully fought parent alienation syndrome.* Retrieved August 12, 2004, from http://www.fact.on.ca/Info/pas/major98.htm

Makin, K. (2008, May 15). Judge rules father brainwashed son into hating mother. *The Globe and Mail.* Retrieved from http://www.theglobeandmail.com.

Mandell, N., & Duffy, A. (1995). *Canadian families: Diversity, conflict and change.* Toronto: Harcourt Brace & Company, Canada.

Massie, H., & Szajnberg, N. (2004). "How could they do that?" Parental aggression: Its impact on children's adult mental health, its link to understanding social violence. In James P. Morgan (Ed.), *Focus on aggression research* (pp. 15-39). New York: Nova Science Publishers, Inc.

McKie, D., Prentice, B., & Reed, P. (1983). *Divorce: Law and the Family in Canada.* Ottawa: Minister of Supply and Services Canada. Statistics Canada Catalogue No. 89-502E.

Millon, T. & Davis, R D. (1996). *Disorders of personality. DSM-IV and beyond* (2nd ed.). New York: Wiley.

Moskowitz, J. (1998). The effect of parental alienation syndrome and interparental conflict on the self-concept of children of divorce (Doctoral dissertation). *ProQuest Information and Learning Company,* (UMI No. 9829488).

Myers, J.E.; Sweeny, T.J.; Witmer, J.M. (2000). The wheel of wellness counseling for wellness: A holistic model for treatment planning. *Journal of Counseling and Development, 78,* 251–266.

National Sleep Foundation (2005). *Summary of findings: 2005 sleep in America poll.* Retrieved June 6, 2005, from http://www.sleepfoundation.org/content/hottopics/2005_summary_of_findings.pdf.

Nielsen, J. (1993). Parental substance abuse and divorce as predictors of injection drug use and high risk sexual behaviors known to transmit HIV. *Journal of Psychology and Human Sexuality, 2,* 29-49.

Pearson, L., & Gallaway, R. (1998). *For the Sake of the Children: Report of the Special Joint Committee on Child Custody and Access.* Ottawa: Parliament of Canada, Public Works and Government Services Canada.

Peterson, J., & Zill, N. (1986). Marital disruption, parent-child relationships, and behavior problems in children. *Journal of Marriage and the Family, 48,* 295-307.

Rand, D. (1997a). The spectrum of parental alienation syndrome (Part I). *American Journal of Forensic Psychology, 15,* 23-51.

Rand, D. (1997b). The spectrum of parental alienation syndrome (Part II). *American Journal of Forensic Psychology, 15,* 39-92.

Raso, C. (2004). If the bread goes stale, it's my dad's fault: The parental alienation syndrome (master's thesis). *ProQuest Information and Learning Company,* National Library of Archives Canada, (0-612-91105-5).

Reay, K.M. (2007). Psychological distress among adult children of divorce who perceive experiencing parental alienation syndrome in earlier years (Doctoral dissertation) *ProQuest Information and Learning Company,* (UMI, 3266272).

Risser, D., Bonsch, A., & Schneider, B. (1996). Family background of drug-related deaths: A descriptive study based on interviews with relatives of deceased drug users. *Journal of Forensic Sciences, 41,* 960-962.

Richardson, C. (1996). Divorce and remarriage. In: M. Baker (Ed.), *Families: Changing trends in Canada* (pp. 233-247). Toronto: McGraw-Hill Ryerson.

Siegel, J., & Langford, J. (1998). MMPI-2 validity scales and suspected parental alienation syndrome. *American Journal of Forensic Psychology, 16,* 5-14.

Seligman, M.E.P., Castellon, C., Cacciola, J., Schulman, P., Luborsky, L., Ollive, M. & Downing, R. (1988). Explanatory style change during cognitive therapy for unipolar depression. *Journal of Abnormal Psychology, 97,* 13-18.

Smith, J. (1991). Aftermath of a false allegation. *Issues in Child Abuse Accusations, 3,* 203.

Stacey, J., & Thorne, B. (1985). The missing feminist revolution in sociology. *Social Problems, 32,* 301-316.

Stahl, P. (1999). Alienation and alignment of children. *California Psychologist, 32,* 23-30.

Statistics Canada. (2002). Changing conjugal life in Canada. *The Daily*, July 12. Retrieved August 21, 2006, from http://www.statcan.ca/Daily/English/020711/do20711a.htm.

Stolberg, A., Camplair, C., Currier, K., & Wells, M. (1987). Individual, familial and environmental determinants of children's post-divorce adjustment and maladjustment. *Journal of Divorce, 13,* 1-22.

Stout, M. (2005). *The sociopath next door: The ruthless versus the rest of us.* New York: Random House, Inc.

Strategic Advantage, Inc. (2003). *The symptom assessment-45 questionnaire (SA-45) technical manual.* Tonawanda, NY: MHS.

Sullivan, M. & Kelly, J. B. (2001). Legal and psychological management of cases with an alienated child. *Family Court Review, 39,* 299-315.

Sun, Y., & Li, Y. (2002). Children's well-being during parents' marital disruption process: A pooled time-series analysis. *Journal of Marriage and Family, 64,* 472-488.

Teachman, J. (2002). Childhood living arrangements and the intergenerational transmission of divorce. *Journal of Marriage and Family, 64,* 717-729.

Turkat, I. (1994). Child visitation interference in divorce. *Clinical Psychology Review, 14,* 737-742.

Turkat, I. (1995). Divorce related malicious mother syndrome. *Journal of Family Violence, 10,* 253-264.

Vassiliou, D. (2001). Parental alienation syndrome: The lost parents' perspective (master's thesis). Retrieved September 12, 2005, from http://www.fact.on.ca/Info/pas/vassil98.htm

Wakefield, H., & Underwager, R. (1990). Personality characteristics of parents making false accusations of sexual abuse in custody disputes. *Issues in Child Abuse Accusations, 2,* 121-136.

Walker, L.G. (2004). Hypnotherapeutic insights and interventions: A cancer odyssey. *Contemporary Hypnosis, 21,* 35-45.

Wallerstein, J. (1985). Children of divorce: Preliminary report of a ten-year follow-up of older children and adolescents. *Journal of the American Academy of Child Psychiatry, 24,* 545-553.

Wallerstein, J. (1991). The long-term effects of divorce on children: A review. *Journal of the American Academy of Child Psychiatry, 30,* 349-360.

Wallerstein, J., & Blakeslee, S. (1989). *Second chances: Men, women, and children a decade after divorce.* New York: Ticknor & Fields.

Wallerstein, J., & Corbin, S. (1989). Daughters of divorce: Report from a ten-year follow-up. *American Journal of Orthopsychiatry, 59,* 593-604.

Wallerstein, J., & Kelly, J. (1980). *Surviving the breakup: How children and parents cope with divorce.* New York: Basic Books.

Warshak, R. (1992). *The custody revolution.* New York: Poseidon Press.

Warshak, R. (2001). Current controversies regarding parental alienation syndrome. *American Journal of Forensic Psychology, 19,* 29-59.

Warshak, R. (2003). Bringing sense to parental alienation: A look at the disputes and the evidence. *Family Law Quarterly, 37,* 273-301.

Warshak, R. (2010a). Family bridges: Using insights from social science to reconnect parents and alienated children. *Family Court Review, 48,* 48-80.

Warshak, R. (2010b). Alienating audiences from innovation: The perils of polemics, ideology, and innuendo. *Family Court Review, 48,* 153-163.

Warshak, R. (2010c). *Divorce poison: How to protect your family from bad-mouthing and brainwashing.* New York: Harper.

Warshak, R. (2011, February). *Welcome back, Pluto: The psychology of families with alienated and estranged children and the...principles, procedures, and ethical considerations of effective help.* Seminar presented by the Psychologists' Association of Alberta, Blackfoot Inn, Calgary, Alberta.

Warshak, R, (Producer & Writer) & Otis, M. (Producer & Writer) (2010a). *Welcome back, Pluto: Understanding, preventing and overcoming parental alienation* [DVD]. United States: Trace Productions for WBP Media.

Warshak, R. & Otis, M. (2010b). Helping alienated children with family bridges: Practice, research, and the pursuit of "humbition". *Family Court Review, 48,* 91-97.

Williams, Justice R. (2001). Should judges close the gate on PAS and PA? *Family and Conciliation Courts Review, 39,* 267-281.

Wolfinger, N. (1998). The effects of parental divorce on adult tobacco and alcohol consumption. *Journal of Health and Social Behavior, 39,* 254-269.

Wolfinger, N. (2005). *Understanding the divorce cycle: The children of divorce in their own marriages.* New York: Cambridge University Press.

Wolpe, J. (1969). *The practice of behavioral therapy.* New York: Pergamon Press Ltd.

Young, J.E. (2002). Schema-focused therapy for personality disorders. In G. Simos (Ed.), *Cognitive Behaviour Therapy: A guide for the practicing clinician* (pp. 201-222). East Sussex: Brunner-Routledge.

CPSIA information can be obtained at www.ICGtesting.com
Printed in the USA
LVOW031645270812

296163LV00004B/2/P